Advance Praise

"Read it and weep, millennials. Philip Klein efficiently demonstrates why it is remarkable that there is not generational conflict. Yet."

—GEORGE F. WILL

"Philip Klein has written a powerful wake-up call to the rising generation. He shows just how badly millennials have been disserved by decades of reckless public policy, but he also offers them some ways forward. This is essential reading for anyone who thinks our politics must care about the future."

—YUVAL LEVIN, author of *The Fractured Republic* and editor of *National Affairs*

"Both political parties in Washington are drunk on debt, and Klein is begging millennials to demand that DC sober up before it's too late. Rather than bashing or ridiculing our generation with lazy stereotypes, *Fear Your Future* offers a rigorous diagnosis of the daunting fiscal challenges on our collective plate. Fellow millennials, please join me in taking a short break from scrolling through Instagram to read this short, digestible book. The clock is ticking, and we're getting screwed."

—GUY BENSON, political editor of Townhall.com and Fox News contributor

"A terrific book. Philip Klein meticulously details the economic challenges faced by millennials—and why more government regulation, debt, and taxes are not the answer."

—BRIAN RIEDL, senior fellow at the
Manhattan Institute

Fear Your Future

FEAR YOUR FUTURE

—— ≽≼ ——

How the Deck Is Stacked against Millennials and
Why Socialism Would Make It Worse

Philip Klein

TEMPLETON PRESS

Templeton Press
300 Conshohocken State Road, Suite 500
West Conshohocken, PA 19428
www.templetonpress.org

Set in Sabon LT Pro 9.9/14.4 by Gopa&Ted2, Inc.

Library of Congress Control Number: 2019949014

ISBN: 978-1-59947-573-8

This paper meets the requirements of ANSI/NISO Z39.48-1992
(Permanence of Paper).
A catalogue record for this book is available
from the Library of Congress.

19 20 21 22 23   10 9 8 7 6 5 4 3 2 1

Printed in the United States of America.

For my son

Contents

Fear Your Future

Introduction

———————— ⊱⊰ ————————

IN EARLY 2018, a large recurring poll of young Americans conducted by the Harvard Kennedy School Institute of Politics asked, "At this moment, would you say that you are more hopeful or fearful about the future of America?" In response, 64 percent—or nearly two-thirds of those aged 18 to 29—said that they were more fearful, compared with just 33 percent who said they were more hopeful.[1]

The abstract concept of the American Dream is often distilled to mean the hope and expectation that the next generation will be better off than their parents. Instead, as millennials[2] transition to adulthood, their generation has been beset with a deep sense of foreboding about the grim future that awaits them.

It would be easy to dismiss this pessimism as a common feature of younger adults facing an uncertain future. Struggling to cope with all the "natural shocks that flesh is heir to" goes back to Shakespeare.[3] Some of the greatest American novels ever published, from "Lost Generation" chroniclers Ernest Hemingway and F. Scott Fitzgerald, explore the dark underbelly of the American Dream. The 1970s—a decade that saw Vietnam, Watergate, rising crime, oil shocks, and stagflation—certainly wasn't a high time for optimism in the United States. Today millennials carry around iPhones in their pockets that have more computing power than all of NASA had in the 1960s when it sent the first men to the moon.[4] Those who take a broader view of the sweep of history, who lived through tumultuous times and witnessed progress, have difficulty producing much sympathy for younger Americans.

As such, millennials may be the most mocked generation in American history. The stereotypes abound. Millennials all think they're special snowflakes. They use social media to deliver play-by-play commentaries on their activities, from shopping for clothes to flossing their teeth. And of course, they have a psychotic obsession with avocado toast.

However, for all the joking directed toward them, millennials have legitimate reasons to be resentful, particularly toward baby boomers.[5] It was the baby boomers who grew up during a massive postwar expansion in America, amassed tremendous wealth, selfishly refused to grapple with any of the nation's serious problems, and left a staggering level of debt and obligations for future generations.

As millennials grow up and try to form families, they will be entering a period in which federal debt will reach the highest sustained levels in American history. Unlike baby boomers, who will avoid the consequences, millennials will have to confront them head on. Absent action, millennials will be staring at a crisis, facing some combination of crushing tax increases, massive inflation, sky-high interest rates, and sudden, significant cuts to retirement programs when they reach their twilight years.

Even though millennials have little reason to believe that retirement programs will deliver what's been promised to them, they are hamstrung in preparing. The reason is that despite recent economic improvement, they were held back by uncontrollable growth in college costs that have saddled them with student debt, even as housing and health care costs have gone up.

As millennials have asserted themselves through popular culture and online media, and exerted more influence politically, the debate surrounding them has become polarizing. Given that millennials tend to be much more liberal, conservatives are often dismissive of their complaints as whining from an overly pampered generation, while those on the Left see an opportunity to steer the younger cohort toward their vision for a more expansive role for government. This book is an attempt to break away from this false dichotomy.

Millennials face twin challenges—chasing rising living costs and absorbing unprecedented federal debt. Politicians have been promising that they can solve the generation's economic woes through massive government programs— free college, free health care, subsidized housing, guaranteed jobs, and so on. But socializing major sectors of the U.S. economy, far from solving millennials' problems, will only make their situation worse by adding to the already unsustainable federal debt that threatens their futures. So yes, millennials face obstacles, but there's a risk that this leads them to make a fatal error by embracing seemingly easy solutions that in reality would irreversibly alter the trajectory of American history.

It doesn't have to end this way. As noted in the last chapter of this book, there are plenty of policy options that could be implemented now to secure the American Dream for future generations. Yet in the current political climate, we are no longer in a position to even have a debate about the various fixes, because both parties have decided it's more convenient to ignore the debt problem. Millennials can change this. By the 2020 election, millennials are expected to surpass baby boomers as the largest adult population,[6] giving them tremendous political influence. Were they to harness that power to demand changes, they could steer the nation toward a different course. But first, they have to wake up to the problem—and rise up.

PART I

———— ⁌ ————

Fear Your Future

CHAPTER ONE

Unprecedented Burden

———— ≥≤ ————

OVER THE COURSE of its history, the United States has had periods in which the federal government has held massive amounts of debt for a relatively short time. There have also been periods in which the government has run manageable deficits for an extended period of time. As they come of age, millennials are inheriting a fiscal situation unlike the one encountered by any previous generation: massive, historically high debt levels, persisting for as far as the eye can see. This is true no matter which way one wants to measure the debt.

Figure 1.1 charts the growth in publicly sold debt as a percentage of the economy ever since George Washington's first term in 1790 and projects it out all the way to 2049, based on data and estimates from the Congressional Budget Office.[1] The long-term trend, up until now, has been that it has spiked during moments of war and economic distress, and then retreated. But what's happening now is markedly different in terms of the magnitude, duration, and circumstances.

Figure 1.1. Federal Debt Held by the Public Since 1790.

Percentage of gross domestic product

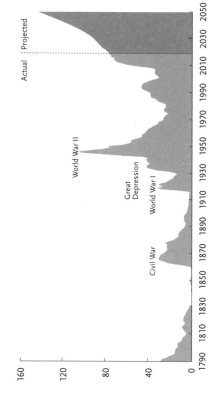

Source: Christine Bogusz, Bo Peery, Benjamin Plotinsky, and Elizabeth Schwinn, eds., *The 2019 Long-Term Budget Outlook* (Congressional Budget Office, 2019), https://www.cbo.gov/system/files/2019-06/55331 -LTBO-2.pdf. Underlying data available for download at the CBO website: https://www.cbo.gov/about /products/budget-economic-data#1.

In the midst of strong economic growth and relative peace, the debt that has been inherited by millennials as a share of the economy is significantly higher than in the aftermath of the Revolutionary War. This was the debt that arguably gave birth to the United States as we know it, as it was one of the factors that forced the nation's founders to abandon the Articles of Confederation in favor of the U.S. Constitution. Figuring out a way to pay the debt became a central part of the legacy of Alexander Hamilton (a plan that has gained modern notoriety for fans of a certain Broadway musical).

The debt being absorbed by millennials also exceeds that which was accumulated during the Civil War, World War I, and the Great Depression. As a result of World War II, there was a massive spike in federal debt in the 1940s as the United States, a late entrant into the war, made up for lost time by energetically ramping up military production. But after the war came to an end within a few years, the debt steadily fell. Unlike the aftermath of World War II, however, the current debt burden won't soon start to retreat.

In 2007, just before the Great Recession and onslaught of baby boomer retirements, public debt was 35 percent of gross domestic product (GDP). It doubled within five years and its upward trajectory has not changed. In the coming decades, it is projected to blow past the highs of the 1940s, reaching unprecedented territory. By the end of the projection period, in 2049, it's supposed to be 144 percent of GDP. Again, what's remarkable is that while previous extraordinary spikes in the debt have come during war and economic turmoil, the current surge in debt is continuing during a time of relative peace and prosperity.

Viewed in dollar terms, as shown in Figure 1.2, the acceleration of public debt from the time the baby boomers entered the workforce to what's projected in the coming decades as millennials take over the workforce is mind-bending. By 2049, debt is projected to be nearly $100 trillion.[2]

Furthermore, by some measures, this actually understates the magnitude of the debt. The CBO data only consider public debt, which does not take into account the government's internal obligations, such as the money exchanged between the U.S. Treasury and the Social Security system. CBO economists argue that the obligations government agencies have to each other are less significant when considering the debt burden, and so instead they focus on the value of all the bonds being issued on publicly traded markets. But others argue that the total debt—or gross debt— provides a truer measure of the nation's overall liabilities.

Looking at Figure 1.3, we can see the total federal debt as a percentage of gross domestic product since 1940. Total debt levels breached an extraordinary 100 percent of gross domestic product while America was fighting World War II. In theory, when debt exceeds 100 percent of GDP, this means that if the value of all the goods and services produced in a country over a given year were exclusively used to pay down the debt, it still wouldn't get rid of all of it. In practice,

FIGURE 1.2. TOTAL PUBLIC FEDERAL DEBT 1964–2049.

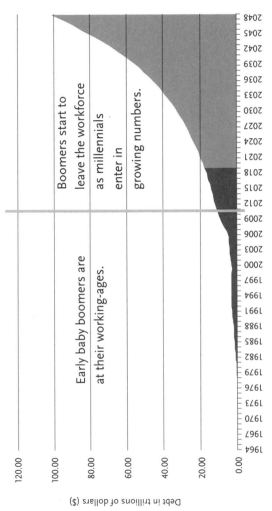

Note: Numbers are projections starting in 2019.

Sources: Years 1964-1968 came from: Christine Bogusz, Leah Mazade, John Skeen, and Christian Spoor, eds., *The Budget and Economic Outlook: Fiscal Years 2004-2013*, (Congressional Budget Office, 2003), Table F-1, 148, https://www.cbo.gov/sites/default/files/108th-congress-2003-2004/reports/entirereport_witherrata.pdf; Years 1969-2018 came from "Historical Budget Data from January 2019," Congressional Budget Office, Table 1. https://www.cbo.gov/about/products/budget-economic-data#2; Projections from 2019 to 2049 came from "Long-Term Budget Projections, Jan. 2019," Congressional Budget Office, Table 1-4, "Annual Data Underlying Key Projections in CBO's Extended Baseline." https://www.cbo.gov/about/products/budget-economic-data#1.

this obviously won't happen as governments, businesses, and individuals need to buy lots of stuff in the meantime. So the nation's policymakers have typically worked toward limiting debt to a sustainable amount. That way, people can continue to live their lives and institutions can make investments, while taxpayers, via government, make reasonable interest payments.

After World War II, as spending returned to more normal levels and the economy took off, the level of debt dwindled. By the time the first baby boomers reached high school graduation age, in 1964, it was cut down to less than half of its wartime peak. By 1974, as early baby boomers were in their 20s and starting to form families, it had fallen to 32.6 percent. In other words, as they entered the workforce, boomers only faced a relatively modest federal debt.

In the following decades, as baby boomers gained political influence and eventually power, they reversed this trend. On one side, Democrats promoted continued growth in the social welfare state. On the other side, Republicans, despite rhetoric about shrinking government, let the cost of the welfare state continue to balloon while pushing through large tax cuts and increasing military spending. This lust for instant gratification took its toll. Instead of leaving the country in the same state as they inherited it, boomers are leaving a nation in financial shambles, with no easy fixes. Despite knowing for decades that a demographic time bomb would get detonated starting in 2011 when the boomers began

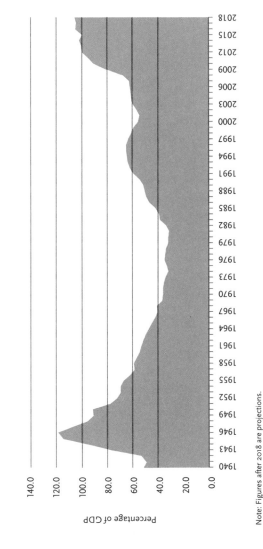

FIGURE 1.3. Gross Debt as Percentage of GDP, 1940–2018.

Note: Figures after 2018 are projections.

Source: "Historical Tables," White House Office of Management and Budget, Table 7.1-Federal Debt at the End of the Year: 1940-2024, https://www.whitehouse.gov/omb/historical-tables/.

to retire, they made sure that nothing was done to reform retirement programs in a way that would have reduced the burden on future generations.

These two factors—mismanagement of the regular budget and failure to do anything about the inevitable long-term problem—saw the debt steadily grow for decades, and then explode in the years following 2008 as the Great Recession coincided with the first wave of retiring baby boomers.

In 2007, total debt as a share of GDP had grown to 62.6 percent. That was historically elevated, but still within the realm of manageable. But by 2012, it had reached 100 percent for the first time since World War II, and has never looked back.

When the early baby boomers were in their working years, total debt averaged 50 percent of GDP. By comparison, since the first millennials turned 18, debt has averaged nearly 80 percent of GDP and has exceeded 100 percent of GDP for seven straight years for the first time in history.

Another way of comparing the debt burden inherited by millennials to the experience of the baby boomers is to try to break the numbers down to the individual level. In Figure 1.4, I've charted the growth in individual median income over time for 25 to 34 year olds against the total federal debt per person since 1974, when the earliest boomers were in their late 20s. At that time, median income was $7,880, whereas the per capita debt was $2,221. That ratio has reversed.

Even though by 2017, median income among 25 to 34

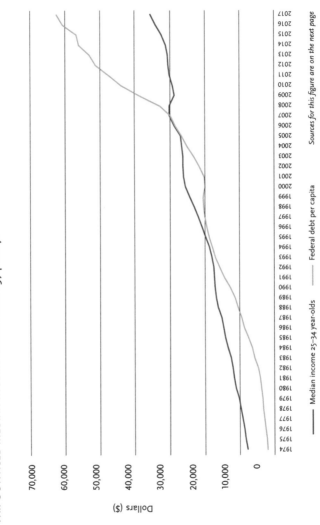

Figure 1.4. For 25–34 Year-Olds, Growth in Their Share of Federal Debt Far Outpaced Median Income Gains from 1974–2017.

Median income 25–34 year-olds   Federal debt per capita   Sources for this figure are on the next page

year olds had grown to $35,455, debt grew much more rapidly, climbing to $62,263 per person. That means that between 1974 and 2017, young Americans' share of the federal debt increased 28 times while their incomes only increased 4.5 times.

This contrast can be seen in Figure 1.5.

Although many would like to blame tax cuts for the accumulation of debt, that isn't supported by the data. To be clear, there is no doubt that if the government were collecting more tax revenue, deficits would be narrower and the debt would not be growing as rapidly. That having been said, it is undeniable from the data that even after the most recent Republican tax cuts signed into law by President Trump in 2017, federal revenues are projected to be above historical levels in the coming decades. In contrast, spending is way out of whack with historical averages, and that's primarily due to growth in Medicare and Social Security, combined with the accompanying spike in interest payments. As CBO puts it, in its projections, "large budget deficits would arise because spending would grow steadily under current law, and

Sources for figures 1.4 and 1.5:"Historical National Population Estimates: July 1, 1900 to July 1, 1999," Census Bureau, last modified June 28, 2000, https://www.census.gov/population/estimates/nation/pop clockest.txt; "National Intercensal Tables: 2000-2010," Census Bureau, last modified November 30, 2016, https://www.census.gov/data/tables/time-series/demo/popest/intercensal-2000-2010-national.html; "Monthly Population Estimates for the United States: April 1, 2010 to December 1, 2019," Census Bureau, published December 2018, https://factfinder.census.gov/faces/tableservices/jsf/pages/productview.xhtml?src=bkmk; "Historical Income Tables: People Table, P-10. Age—People (Both Sexes Combined) by Median and Mean," Census Bureau, last modified August 28, 2018, https://www.census.gov/data/tables/time-series/demo/income-poverty/historical-income-people.html; "Historical Debt Outstanding-Annual 1950–1999," U.S. Treasury Department, https://www.treasurydirect.gov/govt/reports/pd/histdebt/histdebt_histo4.htm; "Historical Debt Outstanding-Annual 2000-2018, U.S. Treasury Department, https://www.treasurydirect.gov/govt/reports/pd/histdebt/histdebt_histo5.htm.

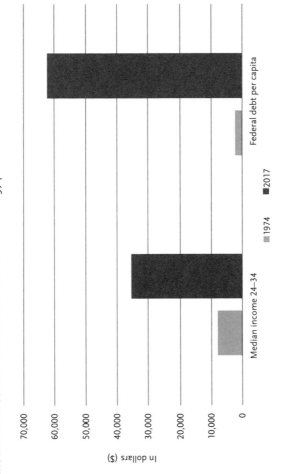

Figure 1.5. Growth in Federal Debt Has Dramatically Outpaced Growth in Incomes for Younger Americans since 1974.

See sources for Figure 1.4.

revenues would not keep pace with that spending growth."[3] In other words, the story of the growing debt is one of taxes not rising fast enough to keep pace with dramatically higher spending, rather than of dramatically lower taxes making modest spending suddenly unaffordable.

As shown in Figure 1.6, tax revenues are currently slightly below the 50-year average of 17.4 percent of GDP, but they are expected to exceed that average by the middle of the coming decade and reach 19.5 percent of GDP by 2049. Thus, if spending were kept in line with the historical average over the past 50 years of 20.3 percent, we'd be looking at nearly a balanced budget in 2049 and there wouldn't be much of a debt problem to worry about. Instead, spending will soar to an astounding 28.2 percent of GDP, substantially above the historical average, resulting in a massive gap that year.

It's also a popular line of argument in some quarters to attribute our debt problem to wasteful military spending. How many times have you heard somebody argue that, if only the Pentagon weren't squandering money, we'd easily be able to support a more generous social safety net? Although no doubt there is waste in the large defense budget, in reality it's social safety net spending—mostly on retirees— that's crowding out defense spending rather than military waste that has forced cuts to social welfare programs.

Figure 1.7 puts core defense spending as a share of GDP up against combined spending on Social Security and Medicare

FIGURE 1.6. SPENDING, NOT INSUFFICIENT TAX REVENUES, ARE DRIVING DEFICITS IN THE COMING DECADES.

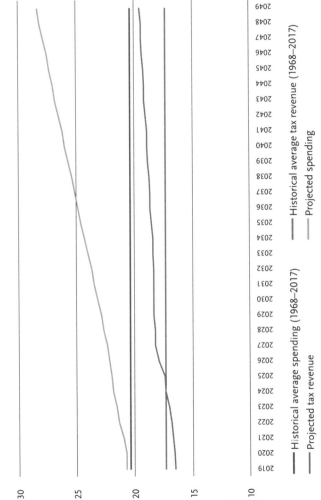

Percentage of GDP

Historical average spending (1968–2017)   Historical average tax revenue (1968–2017)
Projected tax revenue   Projected spending

Sources: "Historical Budget Data, April 2018," Congressional Budget Office, Table 1, https://www.cbo.gov/about/products/budget-economic-data#2; "Long-Term Budget Projections, June 2019, Summary Extended Baseline," Congressional Budget Office, https://www.cbo.gov/about/products/budget-economic-data#1.

starting in 1969 and projected out to 2029. What it shows is a steady decline in defense spending over the decades, but for the ramp up in the wake of the September 11 attacks. In contrast, spending on Social Security and Medicare has continued to eat up a larger and larger share of our economic output, a trend that accelerated after boomers reached Medicare eligibility age in 2011.

The increases in underlying spending and the resulting debt payments are also expected to substantially increase the amount of the budget that will have to be taken up by interest payments, which don't actually provide any benefits. As shown in Figure 1.8, about 9 percent of overall spending is expected to go to interest payments in 2019. By 2049, that will rise to 20 percent, according to CBO projections. That means that one-fifth of the budget would be eaten up by creditors before the federal government paid for a single good or service.

The clear driver of the massive expansion in debt is retirement programs to fund the baby boomers. As the CBO explained the debt problem:

> In particular, over the next 30 years, spending as a share of GDP would increase for Social Security, the major health care programs (primarily Medicare), and interest on the government's debt. In CBO's projections, most of the spending growth for Social Security and Medicare results from the aging of the

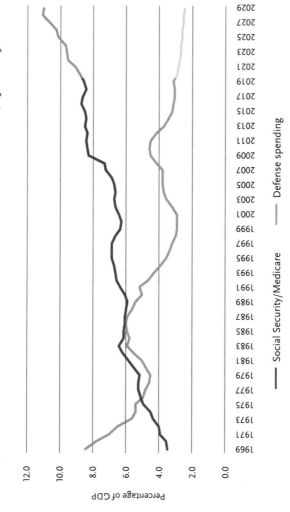

FIGURE 1.7. DEFENSE SPENDING VS. SOCIAL SECURITY AND MEDICARE SPENDING, 1968–2029.

—— Social Security/Medicare   —— Defense spending

Numbers are projections starting in 2019.

Sources: For years 1969 to 2018: "Historical Budget Data, January 2019," Congressional Budget Office, Table 4 (Discretionary Outlays), Table 5 (Mandatory Outlays), https://www.cbo.gov/about/products/budget-economic-data#2; For years 2019-2029, "10-Year Budget Projections, May 2019," Congressional Budget Office, Table 3-1 (CBO's Baseline Projections of Outlays), https://www.cbo.gov/about/products/budget-economic-data#3.

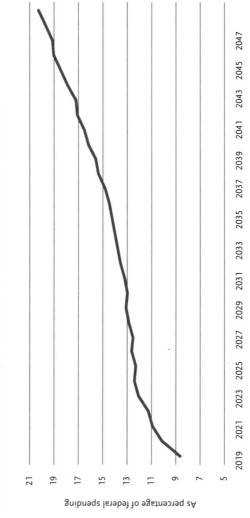

Figure 1.8. Interest Payments Will Take Up Increasing Share of Spending.

As percentage of federal spending

Source: "Long-Term Budget Projections, June 2019," Congressional Budget Office, https://www.cbo.gov/about/products/budget-economic-data#1.

population: As members of the baby-boom generation (people born between 1946 and 1964) age and
as life expectancy continues to rise, the percentage
of the population age 65 or older will grow sharply,
boosting the number of beneficiaries of those programs. Growth in spending on Medicare and the
other major health care programs is also driven by
rising health care costs per person.[4]

The burden of the nation's retirement programs on the
millennial working-age population is significantly higher
than it was when baby boomers were in their main working
years. In 1968, when the earliest boomers would have been
at college graduation age, Medicare was in its infancy, having been passed into law just three years earlier. At the time,
as shown in Figures 1.9 and 1.10, the two major retirement
programs, Social Security and Medicare, accounted for 15.8
percent of the federal budget. In 2018, the share had soared
to 40 percent.

Unlike the World War II spike, however, the current debt
isn't the result of a single major event that's going to end in
a few years and allow the nation to return to fiscal normalcy.
Baby boomers started retiring in 2011, will continue retiring
into the 2030s, and will still be collecting benefits for decades
after that.

There has been a long-standing debate in American politics about the merits and drawbacks of redistributing wealth

FIGURE 1.9. RETIREMENT PROGRAMS AS A SHARE OF SPENDING 1968–2028

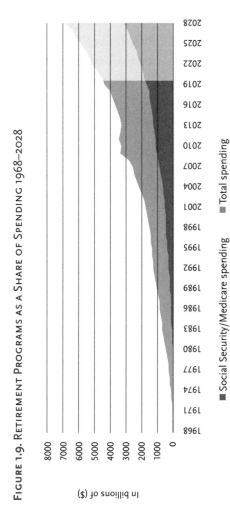

■ Social Security/Medicare spending   ■ Total spending

Note: Numbers are projections starting in 2019.

Sources: "Historical Budget Projections, April 2018," Congressional Budget Office, https://www.cbo.gov/about/products/budget-economic-data #11; "10-Year Budget Projections, May 2019," Congressional Budget Office, https://www.cbo.gov/about/products/budget-economic-data#3.

from the rich to the poor. But the reality is that America does not redistribute wealth from the rich to the poor as much as it redistributes wealth from the young to the old.

One of the major defenses of baby boomers is rooted in the idea that they simply are "taking out what they put into the system." But this idea rests on two popular myths about the way retirement programs operate.

FIGURE 1.10. MEDICARE AND SOCIAL SECURITY AS SHARE OF FEDERAL BUDGET 1968 VS. 2017.

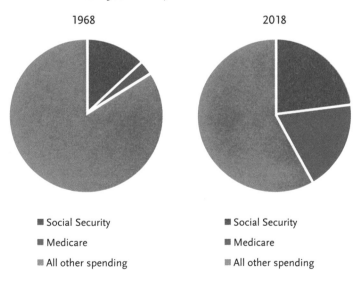

1968

2018

- Social Security
- Medicare
- All other spending

- Social Security
- Medicare
- All other spending

Sources: "Historical Budget Projections, April 2018," Congressional Budget Office, https://www.cbo.gov/about/products/budget-economic-data#11 ; "10-Year Budget Projections, May 2019," Congressional Budget Office, https://www.cbo.gov/about/products/budget-economic-data#3.

The first popular myth is that people pay payroll taxes while they are working, and then that money is put into some sort of government account, saved until their retirement, and then used to pay their retirement benefits. In reality, the payroll taxes of current workers are being used to cover the benefits of those who are currently retired. Thus, millennials will be paying for baby boomers' retirement benefits for the rest of their working lives.

The second myth is that younger generations are simply "paying it forward," just as older generations did for retirees when they were young. In this formulation, baby boomers may not literally be withdrawing from some sort of government savings account they've been putting money into all these years, but they are at least just taking out what they put in to fund the system when they were working and paying payroll taxes. This is also a misconception. In most cases, baby boomers will be collecting a lot more in benefits than they paid in taxes.

The liberal Urban Institute has a report that looks at the expected lifetime value of Social Security and Medicare taxes and benefits for baby boomers who reached 65 in 2015. In Table 1.1, I've listed the estimates for a range of income levels and household characteristics. Just to look at some examples, a single man at the mid-income level of $51,300 would have paid $351,000 in taxes over his working life, but stands to collect $493,000 in lifetime Medicare and Social Security benefits. A married single-earner couple with income of

TABLE 1.1 EXPECTED VALUE OF LIFETIME SOCIAL SECURITY AND MEDICARE TAXES AND BENEFITS FOR THOSE WHO TURNED 65 IN 2015

	LIFETIME TAXES	LIFETIME BENEFITS
Single man with earnings of $23,100	$157,000	$377,000
Single man with earnings of $51,300	$351,000	$493,000
Single man with earnings of $82,100	$556,000	$589,000
Single man with earnings of $127,200	$790,000	$671,000
Single woman with earnings of $23,100	$429,000	$157,000
Single woman with earnings of $51,300	$351,000	$558,000
Single woman with earnings of $82,100	$556,000	$664,000
Single woman with earnings of $127,200	$790,000	$754,000
Married one-earner couple with earnings of $23,100	$157,000	$733,000
Married one-earner couple with earnings of $51,300	$351,000	$931,000

Table continues on next page

TABLE 1.1 (CONTINUED)		
Married one-earner couple with earnings of $82,100	$556,000	$1,093,000
Married one-earner couple with earnings of $127,200	$790,000	$1,231,000
Married couple with two earning total of $46,200	$316,000	$807,000
Married couple with two earning total of $102,600	$701,000	$1,053,000

Source: Eugene Steuerle and Caleb Quakenbush, Social Security and Medicare Lifetime Benefits and Taxes: 2017 Update (Washington, DC: Urban Institute, 2018), Tables 1–13, https://www.urban.org/research/publication/social-security-and-medicare-lifetime-benefits-and-taxes-2017-update/view/full_report.

$82,100 would have paid about $556,000, but can expect to extract nearly double that—$1,093,000.

Only at the highest income levels subject to Social Security payroll tax does the ratio change. For instance, a single man with earnings of $127,200 would have paid $790,000 in taxes and collected $671,000 in benefits.

The demographic reality is that when baby boomers were the bulk of the workforce, they not only had a larger working-age population with whom to share the burden of caring for retirees, but they simultaneously had fewer retirees for whom to care.

Looking at Figures 1.11A and B, we can see how the size of the working-age population has compared with the over

65 population, and how that is expected to change over time. In 1970, when the earlier baby boomers were working but younger ones were still children, those aged 18 to 64 made up 55.9 percent of the total U.S. population, compared with 9.8 percent who were 65 or over. In 2010, the year before the first baby boomers reached retirement age, the working-age population had peaked at just a hair under 62 percent, as the 65 and over population swelled to 15.2 percent. Over time, as the working-age population retreats with baby boomers retiring from the workforce, the number of those over 65 is expected to increase significantly further. By 2030, more than one-in-five Americans will be over 65, and the working-age population will have dipped below 60 percent.

This change is expected to contribute to the strain on the Social Security system, which is projected to see a steady decline in the number of workers supporting every beneficiary. As shown in Figure 1.12, in 2000, when boomers were still in the workforce, there were 3.4 workers per beneficiary. By 2035, under the mid-range estimates of the program's trustees, there will be just 2.3.

The explosion in the retirement aged population is a result not merely of more baby boomers reaching retirement age each year, but also of retirees living longer. When considering this issue, it's preferable to look at life expectancy after 65 as opposed to life expectancy at birth. The average age of life expectancy at birth is driven down by those who die young from causes such as illness, accidents, or violence. It

FIGURE 1.11A. THE PERCENTAGE OF 18 TO 64 YEAR OLDS IS EXPECTED TO DECLINE AS A PERCENTAGE OF THE U.S. POPULATION.

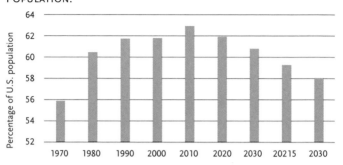

FIGURE 1.11B. AS THE SHARE OF THOSE 65 AND OVER GOES UP.

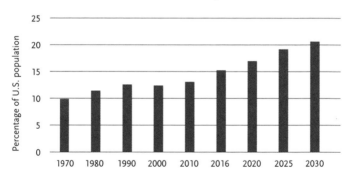

Sources: For years 1970-2019: Lindsay M. Howden and Julie A. Meyer, *Age and Sex Composition*: 2010 (Washington, DC: U.S. Census Bureau, 2011), Figures 4, 6, https://www.census.gov/prod/cen2010/briefs/c2010br-03.pdf; For years 2016, 2020-2030: "2017 National Population Projections Tables," U.S. Census Bureau, Table 2, Projected age and sex composition of the population, https://www.census.gov/data/tables/2017/demo/popproj/2017-summary-tables.html.

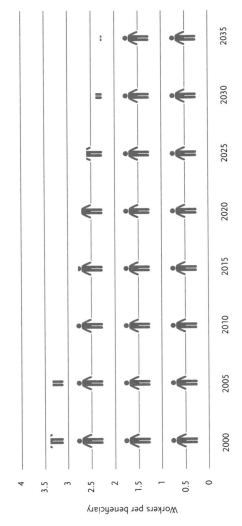

FIGURE 1.12. SOCIAL SECURITY HAS A DECLINING NUMBER OF WORKERS RELATIVE TO BENEFICIARIES.

Note: Numbers are projected starting in 2020.

Source: *The 2019 Annual Report of the Board of Trustees of the Federal Old-Age and Survivors Insurance and Federal Disability Insurance Trust Funds*, published April 25, 2019, Table IV.B3 https://www.ssa.gov/OACT/TR/2019/index.html.

therefore doesn't tell us what we want to know, which is how long the typical person is expected to be collecting retirement benefits. From Figure 1.13, we see that for both sexes, the life expectancy at 65 went from 15.2 years in 1970 to 19.4 years in 2017. Although four years may not seem like a lot, multiplied by 52.7 million (and growing) Social Security beneficiaries[5] and nearly 60 million (and growing) Medicare beneficiaries[6], it represents a massive amount of money.

Although Medicare and Social Security have been discussed together thus far, it's important to note that the programs have distinct fiscal features. Whereas the cost growth of Social Security is driven by the increase in the retirement population, Medicare growth is not only affected by this, but also by the soaring costs of health care. As a result, it's a much more complicated problem to address.

In the past several decades, the cost of health care in the United States has undergone dramatic growth, easily outpacing the expansion of the economy during the same time period. No matter the measurement, the overall trend is one of a massive consumption of health care services.

As shown in Figure 1.14, in 1970, total national health expenditures were $378 billion, adjusted for inflation to 2017 dollars. By 2017, they had reached nearly $3.5 trillion.

Broken down to the individual level in Figure 1.15, we see that the spending on health care went from $1,797 per person to $10,739. In other words, spending increased six times from the time that baby boomers were starting out

FIGURE 1.13. LIFE EXPECTANCY AT AGE 65 (1970 vs. 2017).

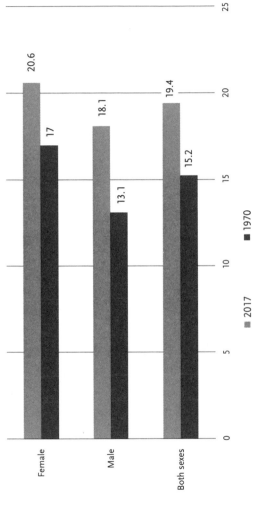

Sources: Sherry L. Murphy, Jiaquan Xu, Kenneth D. Kochanek, and Elizabeth Arias, *Mortality in the United States, 2017*, Centers for Disease Control and Prevention, Nov. 2018. https://www.cdc.gov/nchs/products/databriefs/db328.htm; "Table 22. Life expectancy at birth, at age 65, and at age 75, by sex, race, and Hispanic origin: United States, selected years 1900–2010," Centers for Disease Control and Prevention, last updated 2011, https://www.cdc.gov/nchs/data/hus/2011/022.pdf.

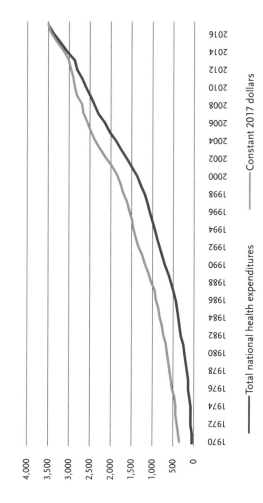

FIGURE 1.14. TOTAL NATIONAL HEALTH EXPENDITURES, U.S. $ PER CAPITA, 1970–2017.

——— Total national health expenditures   ——— Constant 2017 dollars

Source: Rabah Kamal and Cynthia Cox, "How Has U.S. Spending on Healthcare Changed Over Time?" Peterson-Kaiser Health System Tracker, published December 10, 2018, https://www.healthsystemtracker.org/chart-collection/u-s-spending-healthcare-changed-time/#item -total-health-expenditures-have-increased-substantially-over-the-past-several-decades_2017.

their careers to now, when millennials are just starting out their careers.

In Figure 1.16, we see that the growth in health care spending has dramatically outpaced the growth of the U.S. economy, going from 6.9 percent of GDP in 1970 to 17.9 percent in 2017.

The combination of these factors—the increase in the retirement age population relative to the working-age population and the rising cost of health care—is what is making Social Security and Medicare so expensive, thus fueling the growth of the historically unprecedented debt that has been dropped on millennials.

Put another way: millennials are going to be taking care of a lot more retirees, at a much greater cost, for a significantly longer period of time, than any previous generation.

FIGURE 1.15. TOTAL NATIONAL HEALTH EXPENDITURES, U.S. ($) PER CAPITA, 1970–2017.

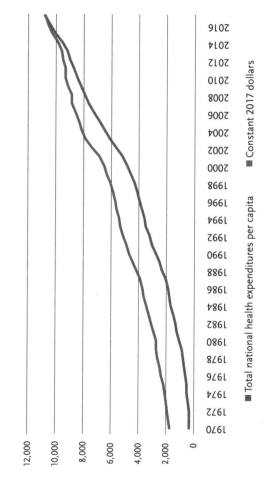

■ Total national health expenditures per capita   ■ Constant 2017 dollars

Source: Rabah Kamal and Cynthia Cox, "How Has U.S. Spending on Healthcare Changed Over Time?" Peterson-Kaiser Health System Tracker, published December 10, 2018, https://www.healthsystemtracker.org/chart-collection/u-s-spending-healthcare-changed-time/#item-on-a-per-capita-basis-health-spending-has-grown-substantially_2017.

FIGURE 1.16. TOTAL NATIONAL HEALTH EXPENDITURES AS A PERCENTAGE OF GROSS DOMESTIC PRODUCT, 1970–2017.

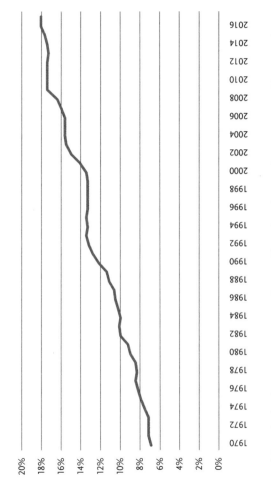

Source: Rabah Kamal and Cynthia Cox, "How Has U.S. Spending on Healthcare Changed Over Time?" Peterson-Kaiser Health System Tracker, published December 10, 2018, https://www.healthsystemtracker.org/chart-collection/u-s-spending-healthcare-changed-time/#item-on-a-per-capita-basis-health-spending-has-grown-substantially_2017.

CHAPTER TWO

The Generational Wealth Gap

≈

To this point, we've focused on the burden millennials are facing in the public sphere as decades of fiscal irresponsibility by the baby boomers failed to prepare the nation for the costs associated with changing demographic realities. But this only tells us part of the story. The next part of it is that at the same time millennials are inheriting an unprecedented level of federal debt, they are also encountering significant headwinds when it comes to their personal finances.

Early baby boomers were fortunate to have entered the workforce during the 1960s, when the economy was undergoing a massive expansion with relatively low unemployment. For millennials, it has been a much different story. The first millennials started entering the workforce in the early 2000s, and they had to navigate the fallout from the bursting of the dot-com bubble and the September 11 attacks. After some better years in the middle of the decade, by 2007, the housing market started to implode, and in the years that followed, another wave of millennials graduated into the worst economy since the Great Depression.

To be sure, a recent Pew Research Center analysis found that with the economy having bounced back from the Great Recession, household income for young adults (aged 23 to 37), which had been lagging in prior generations, reached $69,000 in 2019, which is the highest for that age group on record, even when adjusted for inflation.[1] That said, the growth in household income is, at least partially, a function of the fact that over time, more women have entered the workforce, and their incomes have gone up. As a 2018 study from the Federal Reserve Board relying on different data noted, "Millennials tend to have lower income than members of earlier generations at comparable ages, although the income of young households has not changed much; the difference likely reflects, in part, the rising labor force participation of women."[2]

This can be seen by looking at Census data breaking down median income for younger *individuals* by sex. As shown in Figure 2.1, measured in constant 2017 dollars, median income of males aged 25 to 34 years old has actually gone down over time. It was $47,128 in 1974, when the early boomers were in their 20s, and it dipped to as low as $35,588 in 2011. Even after recovering from the Great Recession, it had only reached $40,575 by 2017—still well off from the boomer era. Women, in contrast, while still earning less than men, have seen incomes go from $20,293 in 1974 to $30,601 in 2017. Looking at the total population without taking into account sex, median income of

FIGURE 2.1. MEDIAN INCOME OF 25–34 YEAR-OLDS (1974–2017).

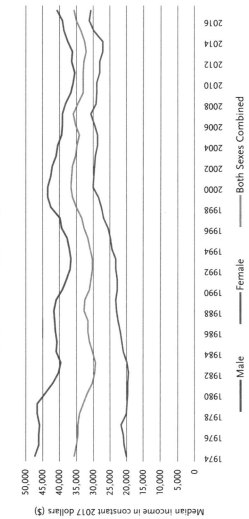

Source: "Historical Income Tables: People," Table P-8. Age – People by Median Income and Sex; Table P-10. Age – People (Both Sexes Combined) by Median and Mean," U.S. Census Bureau, last modified August 28, 2018, https://www.census.gov/data/tables/time-series/demo/income-poverty/historical-income-people.html.

individuals has been stagnant—it was $35,426 in 1974 and $35,455 in 2017.

What's happened, however, is that the existence of more dual income households compared with a few decades ago has helped drive up household income. In 1970, according to Pew, 49 percent of families with children under 18 had dual incomes, but that rose to 66 percent by 2015.[3]

Another consequence of having two-income families is that when millennials choose to have kids, they are more reliant on expensive child care than previous generations. In 2018, a survey by Care.com found that the national average annual cost of child care was $28,354 for a nanny and $9,589 for a daycare center, but that amount escalates in large cities such as New York.[4] The survey found that one in three families report paying 20 percent or more of their household income on child care.[5] Even if daycare doesn't necessarily erase all of the added income coming in to two-income families, it certainly eats into it.

This is part of a much larger issue: despite the income gains of recent years, a combination of the difficult timing of their entry into the workforce and rising costs of living have made it significantly more difficult for millennials to build wealth and save for their life goals than for those who came before them.

It's true that when taking into account total compensation including benefits, the numbers would look better. But this also reflects the fact that workers have had to accept lower wage growth than they otherwise would have in exchange for health insurance benefits, which cost employers more given the increase we've seen in the cost of health care.

In theory, Obamacare was supposed to make insurance more accessible to millennials and address rising health care costs (hence the "Affordable Care Act" name). But in practice, it's just another example of a government program that asks younger Americans to help subsidize the costs of older Americans.

One of the most popular parts of Obamacare is the provision that makes it illegal for insurers to deny coverage to those with pre-existing conditions or to charge more on the basis of health status. Somewhat relatedly, the law limits how much more insurers can charge older individuals. It also requires that insurers cover a raft of government-mandated benefits. Although this comprehensive coverage has been helpful for those near retirement with serious health conditions who previously had difficulty obtaining insurance, it has meant that insurers have had to offset medical losses by jacking up premiums on younger and healthier individuals with limited medical needs.

For younger Americans seeking insurance, Obamacare requires them to pay more so that older Americans can pay less and makes them purchase more comprehensive insurance policies than they need so that older Americans can have broader coverage.

To get a sense of how Obamacare's distorted subsidy

structure disadvantages millennials, take the example of two adults, one 60 years old, and the other 30 years old, each earning $40,000. Under the law, the 60-year-old would receive an estimated $687 per month in subsidies, making it possible to purchase a mid-tier "silver" plan for $329, or a more basic "bronze" plan for $36 per month. In contrast, the 30-year-old with the same income would get just $96 per month in financial help. Although the "silver" plan would cost the same, a "bronze" plan would cost that millennial $206 per month. That means that under Obamacare, millennials could pay nearly six times as much for the same plan as somebody older with the same income, despite having much lower medical costs.[6]

In addition to health care costs, the drastic run up in housing prices in the past several decades, even after the 2007 collapse, has made it difficult for millennials to afford homes.

As seen in Figure 2.2, in 1974, when the first baby boomers were 28, the median sale price of a house was $37,200. In 2017, the price had multiplied more than nine times to $337,900. Yet median income only went up 4.5 times during that same time period.

One of the reasons why houses have gotten more expensive is that they have gotten much bigger. Between 1973 and 2015, the square-footage of the median house soared 62 percent, according to an analysis by Mark J. Perry of the American Enterprise Institute, from 1,525 square feet to a whopping 2,467 square feet. What's incredible is that at the same time the size of houses went up, the number of people

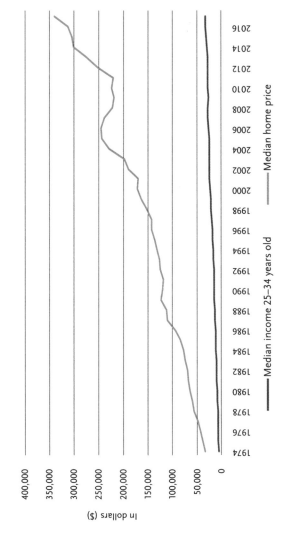

FIGURE 2.2. MEDIAN HOME PRICE VS. MEDIAN INCOME OF 25–34 YEAR OLDS (1974–2017).

Sources: "Historical Income Tables: People," Census Bureau, Table P-10. Age – People (Both Sexes Combined) by Median and Mean. https://www.census.gov/data/tables/time-series/demo/income-poverty/historical-income-people.html; U.S. Census Bureau and U.S. Department of Housing and Urban Development, "Median Sales Price of Houses Sold for the United States [MSPUS]," Federal Reserve Bank of St. Louis; https://fred.stlouisfed.org/series/MSPUS, April 29, 2019.

living in each house went down. So over the same period, the living space per person nearly doubled, from 507 square feet to 971 square feet.[7]

The positive way of looking at this is to say that the price per square foot hasn't actually changed much over time— that is, people are paying more for houses, but they're also getting more space. However, as we'll see later in the chapter, contrary to stereotype, millennials are in many ways more practical-minded than previous generations. So those younger potential house hunters who are willing to settle for something smaller just to get a foothold in the housing market are having a more difficult time finding starter homes.

In 2019, the *Wall Street Journal* picked up on the problem of the excess supply of absurdly large houses from an alternate angle. "Many baby boomers poured millions into these spacious homes, planning to live out their golden years in houses with all the bells and whistles," the *Journal* reported. "Now, many boomers are discovering that these large, high-maintenance houses no longer fit their needs as they grow older, but younger people aren't buying them."[8]

Given the difficulty of finding affordable houses, it's no surprise that the home ownership rate among younger Americans has declined substantially. A study from the Stanford Center on Longevity found that at age 30, 48.3 percent of baby boomers owned their own homes, but that number had dropped to 35.8 percent among early millennials when they hit 30.[9]

Figure 2.3 compares the home ownership rate among the two generations at every age from 25 to 35. Though it's based on a separate study from the Center for Retirement Research at Boston College and focuses only on late boomers (those born between 1954 to 1964), the overall trend is the same—at every age, the home ownership rate is lower among millennials.[10]

Unfortunately for millennials, the rental market hasn't gotten any more affordable, either. As Figure 2.4 shows, on an inflation-adjusted basis, median rent (including utilities) jumped 46 percent between 1970 and 2017, according to an analysis of Census data, from a monthly rate of $694 to $1,012.

One significant obstacle to the building of more affordable housing has been a raft of regulations imposed by local governments including zoning laws, land-use restrictions, and onerous building permitting processes. A 2018 Department of Housing and Urban Development review of the evidence found that "research suggests that more highly regulated jurisdictions tend to have higher housing prices, with regulations discouraging new development or making it less dense while making the housing that is built more expensive."[11]

In addition to the sheer cost of housing, a significant reason why home ownership rates have declined is that millennials are having to defer major life decisions, like purchasing a house, because of the 800-pound gorilla in the room: they are saddled with an incredible amount of student debt as a

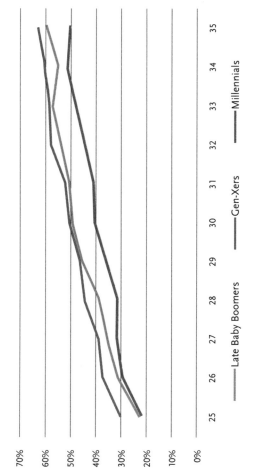

FIGURE 2.3 PERCENTAGE OF HOUSEHOLDS WHO OWN A HOME, AGES 25–35.

Source: Alice H. Munnell and Wenliang Hou, *Will Millennials Be Ready for Retirement?* Center for Retirement Research, published January 2018, https://crr.bc.edu/briefs/will-millennials-be-ready-for-retirement/.

FIGURE 2.4. MEDIAN GROSS RENT IN U.S. 1970–2017 (IN CONSTANT 2017 DOLLARS).

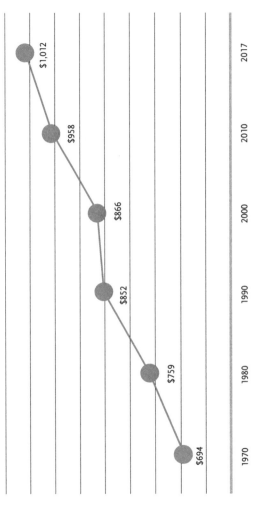

Note: Inflation calculations by author based on CPI-U, via the Bureau of Labor Statistics CPI Inflation Calculator. https://www.bls.gov/data/inflation_calculator.htm.

Sources: For 1970–2000: "Median Gross Rents: Unadjusted," U.S. Census Bureau, https://www2.census.gov/programs-surveys/decennial/tables/time -series/coh-grossrents/grossrents-unadj.txt; For 2010 and 2017: "American Community Survey 1-Year Estimates: Median Gross Rents (Dollars), U.S. Census Bureau, https://factfinder.census.gov/faces/tableservices/jsf/pages/productview.xhtml?pid=ACS_17_1YR_B25064&prodType=table.

result of the runaway increase in college costs over the past several decades.

The recent college admissions scandal, in which wealthy and celebrity parents committed fraud to get their children into colleges to protect their own social status, was an extreme but natural progression of a trend that has elevated the importance of higher education (or at least the value of selective schools) beyond any reasonable level of worth.

Baby boomers graduated from high school at a time when the economy had more opportunities for well-paying jobs that did not require college degrees or special credentials. As researcher Lyman Stone of the Institute for Family Studies has written, "Laws and rules requiring workers to have special licenses, degrees, or certificates to work have proliferated over the past few decades. And while much of this rise came before Boomers were politically active, instead of reversing the trend, they extended it."[12]

A study Stone did for the American Enterprise Institute saw an explosion in licensing requirements in the past several decades.

> As America has aged, our labor rules have become less flexible. A young American cannot just pick up and become an auctioneer if they want to: 30 states require a license, and many of those have a minimum age requirement. Further, an auctioneer's license costs around $160 and may require over

50 hours of training. All of that is required, just to be able to sell things at auction. Louisiana even requires a license for a person to be a florist, complete with an exam and a nearly $200 fee.[13]. . . By privileging existing workers, licensure rules increase income inequality, and they do so specifically by shifting income toward *older* workers. . . . Jobs that once required a high-school degree now require a college degree.[14]

When the boomers were coming of age, not only were there more opportunities for decent paying jobs that didn't require a college degree, but those who chose to go to college were able to do so for significantly less money.

Figures 2.5 and 2.6 chart the extraordinary growth in college costs from the 1971–72 school year to the most recent 2018–19 year. The cost of a single year at private institutions soared from $11,330 to $35,830 in inflation adjusted 2018 dollars, representing an increase of 216 percent. At public institutions, the cost rose from $2,660 to $10,230 over that time period—representing a 285 percent increase.

To put things in perspective, this means that in 1971–72, a student could work an average of seven hours a week over the course of the year at the equivalent of the current federal minimum wage and gross enough before taxes to cover tuition and fees at a public university. To accomplish the same today, a student would have to work 27 hours a week. It

FIGURE 2.5. TUITION AND FEES, PRIVATE NONPROFIT FOUR-YEAR COLLEGES (IN 2018 DOLLARS).

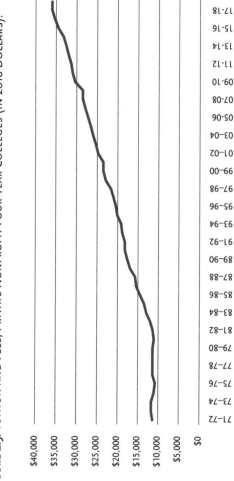

Source: "Table 2: Average Tuition and Fees and Room and Board (Enrollment-Weighted) in Current Dollars and in 2018 Dollars, 1971–72 to 2018–19," College Board, https://trends.collegeboard.org/college-pricing/figures-tables/tuition-fees-room-and-board-over-time.

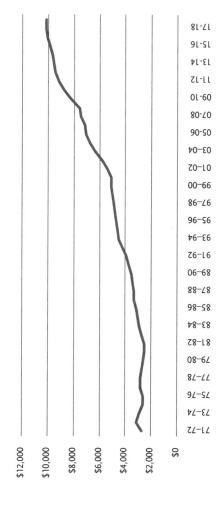

FIGURE 2.6. TUITION AND FEES, PUBLIC FOUR-YEAR COLLEGES (IN 2018 DOLLARS).

Source: "Table 2: Average Tuition and Fees and Room and Board (Enrollment-Weighted) in Current Dollars and in 2018 Dollars, 1971–72 to 2018–19, College Board," https://trends.collegeboard.org/college-pricing/figures-tables/tuition-fees-room-and-board-over-time.

would take an insane 95 hours a week to cover the costs of attending a private university.[15]

Given this stunning growth and how daunting it is for students to make much of a dent in their tuition payments through part-time work, it's no surprise that in recent decades they have begun to pile on an incredible amount of student debt.

Figure 2.7 tracks new student loans made each year from federal and nonfederal sources, in constant 2017 dollars. The data, from the College Board, shows the value went from $7 billion during the 1970–71 academic year, to $96 billion in 2015–16—an increase of a ridiculous 1,271 percent. Again, this is adjusted for inflation.

A separate study from the Pew Research Center calculated that growth in annual student borrowing increased a staggering 352 percent from 1990–91 to 2012–13, even though the total number of students rose just 62 percent during the same time period.[16]

These annual increases in new loans have added up, and the growth in cumulative student loan debt has soared since the turn of the century, as shown in Figure 2.8. In 2001, there were $340 billion[17] in student loans outstanding, and that number has continued to grow at an alarming rate. At the start of 2006, there were $481 billion in loans outstanding, but that more than tripled, to $1.57 trillion, by the end of 2018.

Student loans have now surpassed credit cards and auto

FIGURE 2.7. ANNUAL STUDENT LOANS (IN CONSTANT 2017 DOLLARS).

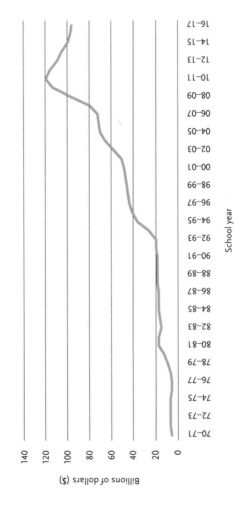

Source: "Trends in Higher Education: Loans, Table 1," College Board, https://trends.collegeboard.org/student-aid/figures-tables/loans.

FIGURE 2.8. CUMULATIVE STUDENT LOAN DEBT (2006–2017).

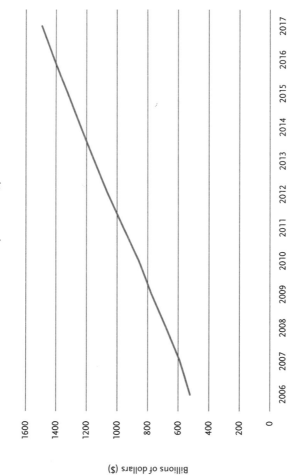

Billions of dollars ($)

Source: "Student Loans Owned and Securitized, Outstanding [SLOAS]," Federal Reserve Bank of St. Louis; https://fred.stlouisfed.org/series/SLOAS.

THE GENERATIONAL WEALTH GAP 59

loans in terms of total value, as shown in Table 2.1, making them the number two source of consumer debt, behind only mortgages, according to Fed data.[18]

TABLE 2.1 U.S. CONSUMER DEBT	
TYPE OF DEBT	AMOUNT IN TRILLIONS OF DOLLARS ($)
Mortgages	9.54
Student loans	1.57
Auto loans	1.15
Credit cards	1.06

Sources: "Consumer Credit – G.19," Board of Governors of the Federal Reserve System, published July 8, 2019, https://www.federalreserve.gov/releases/g19/Current/; "Household Debt and Credit Report," Federal Reserve Bank of New York, https://www.newyorkfed.org/microeconom ics/hhdc.html; "Mortgage Debt Outstanding, All Holders," Federal Reserve Bank of St. Louis, last modified June 10, 2019, https://fred.stlouisfed.org/series/MDOAH; "Motor Vehicle Loans Owned and Securitized, Outstanding," Federal Reserve Bank of St. Louis, last modified July 8, 2019, https://fred.stlouisfed.org/series/MVLOAS; "Student Loans Owned and Securitized, Outstanding," Federal Reserve Bank of St. Louis, last modified July 8, 2019, https://fred.stlouisfed .org/series/SLOAS#0.

This understates the magnitude of the problem for millennials. By the end of 2018, student loan debt had grown to be nearly 50 percent higher than credit card debt. But as the Nilson Report, a publication covering the credit card industry, observed, unlike credit card debt, which is held by the entire adult population, student loan debt is primarily concentrated among younger Americans.[19]

A 2016 Pew analysis found that overall, 37 percent of those aged 18 to 29 had student debt, and 22 percent of those aged 30 to 44 did. Yet just 7 percent of those aged 45 to 59 were carrying student debt and 2 percent of those 60 and over had the loans.[20]

Another analysis of Federal Reserve data from the Center for Retirement Research at Boston College found that significantly fewer baby boomers carried student loan debt even looking at both groups when they were younger. In 1989, 22 percent of those aged 22 to 35 (i.e. late baby boomers) carried student loan debt. Though data is not available before 1989, it's safe to assume, based on the overall student loan origination data we already looked at, that the percentage for early baby boomers would have been lower. Even compared with late boomers, however, the contrast is stark, as 46 percent of those aged 22 to 35 carried debt in 2016, according to this study. This also doesn't take into account that, given the significantly cheaper cost of college, balances would have been much smaller decades ago for those who did have debt.[21]

Ironically, there is a growing body of evidence[22] suggesting that the efforts of lawmakers to increase the number of Americans with college degrees by expanding student loan programs has actually fueled the dramatic increase in college costs. For instance, a 2016 National Bureau of Economic Research working paper looked at the rise in tuition between 1987 and 2010, and found that policies to make student loan programs more generous could "fully account" for the tuition increase.[23] Though its model could exaggerate the impact of federal student loans alone (something the authors themselves acknowledge), the overall economic logic is pretty straightforward. Businesses set prices based on demand and consumers' ability to pay. If the government subsidizes something considerably, it increases consumers' demand and ability to pay. In this case, the expansion of federal student loan programs allowed colleges to increase tuition more than they otherwise would have been able to, thus creating a vicious circle. The more student loans are subsidized, the more colleges can hike tuition, and then the more need there is for student loans.

Whatever the cause, the reality for many millennials has been that they've had to enter the workforce with a soul-crushing amount of debt. In 2016–17, according to College Board data, 59 percent of graduates with bachelor's degrees had student debt, and the average amount was $16,700. Nearly one of five borrowers had a balance exceeding $40,000.[24] To provide some perspective, assuming a 5 percent interest rate, if graduates with that amount of debt were to pay $400 a month, it would take them nearly 11 years to pay off the debt, and they would have spent close to an additional $12,000 on interest during that time.

It is true that some studies have shown that individuals

with college degrees earn more than $1 million more over the course of their lifetimes than those with just high school degrees.[25] So for all the mocking about the worthlessness of a college degree, many have argued that over the course of a lifetime, the degree more than pays for itself. However, it's also true that the sample here is a bit skewed. In the current system, the high school graduates who go on to college tend to be better students and more ambitious than those who do not, so we have no idea what their earnings would be like had they skipped college and gone directly into the workforce and learned on the job. Furthermore, as already noted, in previous generations there were more well-paying jobs available to those without college degrees.

In 2017, Australian real estate magnate Tim Gurner garnered international attention when he spoke about the difficulties that younger people have had purchasing their own homes and said, "When I was trying to buy my first home, I wasn't buying smashed avocado for $19 and four coffees at $4 each."[26] The remarks spread like wildfire around the world, generating headlines such as, "Millionaire to Millennials: Your avocado toast addiction is costing you a house."[27] Though this was the source of great fun on the Internet, it was evocative of the overall stereotype of millennials as entitled and profligate. But are millennials really squandering their future over bottomless mimosa brunches?

The science of studying millennials' financial habits is tricky, as researchers are working to make sense of a moving target, and key data often lags by several years. Also, as noted earlier, many millennials entered the workforce in the teeth of the Great Recession, and as of now, it may be too early to tell which observable tendencies in millennials are merely a short-term reaction to this dramatic event, and which ones are more permanent characteristics. All of this having been said, the available data and surveys provide ample evidence that, far from being reckless, millennials are in many ways behaving in a much more practical and disciplined manner financially than prior generations at similar ages. At the same time, the mounting burdens of student loan debt and higher living costs are making it difficult for them to gain financial traction.

In recent years, there have been a spate of headlines about millennials' aversion to credit after having been scarred by the experience of the Great Recession as well as tales of previous generations being buried in credit card debt. But the reality is more complex. In truth, they have been employing credit in new and interesting ways that provide some insight into how they view money.

You may have read some of the stories about millennials' hatred for credit cards.[28] Though there is definitely some truth to this, the data show this narrative is a bit overstated as well as dated. Every three years beginning in 1989, the Federal Reserve Board's Survey of Consumer Finances has tracked credit card debt among different age groups. As shown in Figure 2.9, in 1989, 44.5 percent of under 35 households carried credit card debt, a number that jumped in the 1990s, reaching a peak of 54.7 percent in 1995. It then held relatively steady until the Great Recession hit, when it dropped to 38.7 percent in 2010 and an all-time low of 36.8 percent in 2013.

This led to a flurry of articles such as one from the *New York Times*, headlined, "How Millennials Became Spooked by Credit Cards."[29] There was certainly a perfect storm of factors that drove down credit card usage among younger Americans. In 2009, Congress passed the "Credit Card Accountability Responsibility and Disclosure Act,"[30] which made it more difficult for card companies to market to individuals under 21. Among other consequences, it effectively got rid of the ubiquitous tents that companies had set up on college campuses at which they handed out t-shirts and gifts to students as inducements to sign up for cards.[31] In addition to regulatory changes, the financial market crash saw banks tighten lending standards, and also trained a younger generation, already saddled with student loans, to be more skittish about piling on debt.

However, in the 2016 Fed survey, the number of under 35 households with credit card debt jumped back up to 45.4 percent. This suggests that although millennials may have been slower to embrace credit than earlier generations in the wake of the recession, as the economy has rebounded and the memory has faded, the downward trend in credit card usage has begun to reverse itself and the gap between

FIGURE 2.9. PERCENTAGE OF UNDER 35 POPULATION WITH CREDIT CARD DEBT.

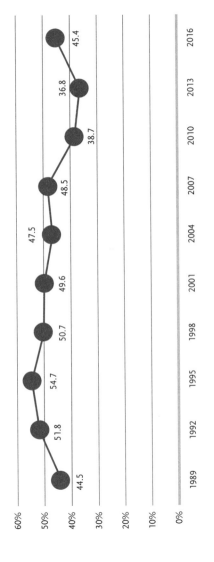

Source: "Survey of Consumer Finances (SCR): Table 13," Board of Governors of the Federal Reserve System, last modified July 23, 2018, https://www.federalreserve.gov/econres/scfindex.htm.

millennials and their predecessors has narrowed. But it's also important to recognize that this has only been true up to a point. Even though the percentage of those in the under 35 crowd holding credit card debt is higher than it was in the wake of the recession, it's still lower than any other year from 1992 to 2007, and far off from its 1995 peak.[32]

It's a similar story when looking at the average amount of credit card debt held by the under 35 age group. At $3,700 in 2016, it isn't the lowest ever recorded, but it's still well off from the pre-recession peak in 2007 of $6,000.[33]

David Robertson, who has covered the credit card industry for decades as publisher of the Nilson Report, described how the entrance of the baby boomers into the workforce coincided with the introduction of unsecured credit and fueled the credit card industry's growth. However, due to the fierce competition, banks developed lax lending standards, which led to some bad habits. Millennials entered the scene when that whole world came crashing down.

"When the baby boomers came up, anybody who could sit up and take nourishment got a credit card," he joked. "Back in the day, mistakes were made and pets were being offered credit. . . . You don't hear those kinds of stories anymore."[34]

He continued,

> For millennials, there's something very different about them. They came up encumbered by debt that has nothing to do with credit cards, and that's stu-

dent loans. . . . So when you talk about baby boomers and the generations that came behind them, the spending power is nowhere near the same . . . the credit limits are nowhere near the same and then even those millennials who have a credit card were so impacted by the Great Recession that they tend to not be the kinds of people who borrow money rather blithely.[35]

What survey after survey has been finding is that millennials are significantly more comfortable using credit when it is for a specific purpose, and they have been much more willing to take out loans that can be paid off in installments. Doing so allows them to get a specific thing that they want, but also enables them to budget for a set monthly payment. This is different from carrying several credit cards in their wallets that could lead them to accumulate debt by charging expenses on an ongoing basis. As seen in Figure 2.10, in 2016, the percentage of the under 35 population with installment loans reached an all-time high of 67.5 percent, according to Fed data.

Innovations in financial technology have made it easier for companies to offer quick approval on personal loans, expanding the use of installment loans beyond classic large purchases such as a new couch or refrigerator, and into smaller items, such as clothing.

The Cincinnati-based Fifth Third Bancorp did extensive

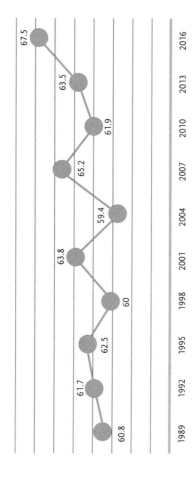

FIGURE 2.10. PERCENTAGE OF UNDER 35 POPULATION WITH INSTALLMENT LOANS.

Source: "Survey of Consumer Finances (SCF): Table 13," Board of Governors of the Federal Reserve System, last modified July 23, 2018, https://www.federalreserve.gov/econres/scfindex.htm.

research on millennials, and as reported by the American Banker, found that, "millennials in particular dislike carrying credit card debt but have little problem taking out a loan to pay for a specific product or service, such as a laptop or a vacation."[36]

This is confirmed by additional survey data. TransUnion, one of the major credit reporting agencies, did an extensive study on millennial finances. As part of it, they compared millennials with Generation X at ages 21 to 34. What they found was the percentage of millennials opening bank-issued credit cards had dropped 22 percent; private label credit card openings had dropped 10 percent; and mortgage loans had dropped 47 percent. On the flip side, the percentage of millennials taking out personal loans nearly doubled.[37]

The study also found that millennials are carrying lower credit card balances, and that "they were almost twice as likely to rank debit cards as their first choice of payment."[38] Debit cards allow millennials to have the convenience offered by credit cards, while the money comes directly out of their bank accounts and thus doesn't involve accruing debt.

A 2018 study from market research and consulting firm Aite asked different generations to describe which statement best represented how they used loyalty and rewards cards. Forty-four percent of millennials answered, "I use one card for all purchases with a specific goal in mind." That compared to 34 percent for baby boomers.[39]

There are also other indications that millennials are being

more deliberate and practical in their spending patterns. For instance, the previously mentioned TransUnion survey found millennials were much more likely to drive around older cars, suggesting that they are more interested in functionality than status relative to earlier generations. Also, they are much less loyal to brands than previous generations, willing to go hunting for cheaper deals and change who they do business with, something observed in the relative frequency with which they switch car insurance carriers. Switching brands is more pragmatic than paying more for a good or service due to an emotional attachment to a specific brand or the simple power of inertia.

Another observable trend is that millennials have been significantly less interested in playing the lottery. Whereas 61 percent of those between the ages of 50 to 64 reported playing the lottery within the previous year, according to a 2016 Gallup poll, only a third of 18 to 29 year olds did. When Reuters reported on the phenomenon in 2017, the wire service quoted a 21-year-old millennial as explaining, "I feel like everything's just too expensive nowadays to just kind of throw away your money on luck."[40]

A broader look at expenses also cuts against the image of millennials as being uniquely irresponsible with money. Though they tend to eat out at restaurants and drink at bars more than older generations, the amount they spend on food, alcohol, and clothing as a percentage of their incomes is consistent with older generations, according to a breakdown of the Bureau of Labor Statistics' Consumer Expenditure Survey from the finance site NerdWallet.[41]

When it comes to their longer-term financial planning, data show that millennials have indicated a desire to save more, but also reveal that they face tremendous difficulty doing so given all of the costs they are juggling, especially student loans.

One 2018 study by life insurer Northwestern Mutual[42] found that 29 percent of millennials said that financial planning makes them feel "excited and inspired," compared with 12 percent of baby boomers. Millennials, at 57 percent, were more likely to say they were "highly disciplined" or "disciplined" financial planners than baby boomers, of which 45 percent said the same. However, the survey found 78 percent of millennials said they felt "pulled apart" to find a balance between current financial responsibilities and future ones, compared with 57 percent of baby boomers who reported having the same struggle. In another indication of how the different generations approach money, 29 percent of millennials said they felt "afraid, uncomfortable, or guilty" spending money even in cases when they could afford to, which compares with just 16 percent of baby boomers who said the same.

Another study released in 2018, this one from NBC/GenForward, reinforced the fact that millennials are feeling financial stress, and showed that the strain is affecting their planning. The survey of those aged 18 to 34 found that 67 percent said they would have at least some difficulty paying a bill of $1,000, with 42 percent saying it would cause them "a lot of difficulty." Additionally, more than half said that debt has caused them to delay major life events. Specifically, 34 percent said it has delayed them buying a home, 31 percent mentioned saving for retirement, and 14 percent said it was forcing them to postpone getting married.[43]

As we saw earlier, the rising cost of housing has made it more difficult for younger Americans to purchase their own homes, but being saddled with student loan debt has made things even more daunting. Navient, an asset management firm, found in a 2017 financial health study of young Americans that just 42 percent of those aged 31 to 35 who still have student debt own a home, which compares with an ownership rate of 61 percent among those graduates who are free of student debt.[44]

Although nearly all young adults aged 22 to 35 reported that they were saving (or at least trying to), the actual reported savings were more discouraging. Specifically, 40 percent have no actual savings, 54 percent have $1,000 or less in savings, and 70 percent have $5,000 or less. Interestingly, 33 percent of those surveyed said they were saving for a specific goal, yet in reality had zero saved.[45]

Looking at retirement specifically, eight out of 10 among the whole age cohort said they either were not saving for retirement, or had no actual money saved. Just 12 percent reported savings of more than $5,000. Even among those aged 34 to 35, who have been in the workforce longer and have had more years to pay off debt, just 15 percent reported retirement savings of over $5,000. There's an old rule of thumb that ideally, people should aim to have twice their salaries in savings by age 35. Just about 4 percent of early millennials in this survey would have met that standard.[46]

As any financial planner would tell you, delaying savings makes it dramatically more difficult to meet retirement goals. People who start saving when they're young can afford to invest more aggressively in stocks and earn higher returns, because they have time to weather the storm of short-term market fluctuations. In addition, they get to maximize the benefits of compound interest. Just to give a basic example, if somebody had $5,000 in savings at age 25 and added $1,000 per year at 5 percent growth, that would turn into $162,039 by age 65. In contrast, if that same person started when they were 35 and added the same amount at the same growth rate, they'd only have $91,370 saved. The accumulation of student loan debt coupled with other rising costs, thus, not only is making life a struggle for millennials now, but it's also making it more likely they won't be sufficiently prepared for retirement.

A series of studies at the Center for Retirement Research at Boston College has been closely tracking the retirement prospects for millennials. Two researchers there, Alicia H. Munnell and Wenliang Hou, concluded in a 2018 study of millennials born from 1981 to 1991 that they were "well behind other cohorts at the same age" when it comes to being prepared for retirement, mainly due to the double whammy of having graduated into a weak labor market and being saddled with student debt.[47] The student debt has a direct effect, by making it more difficult to save for retirement, but also an indirect effect, by making millennials delay other life events such as purchasing a home.

As we have seen earlier, the home ownership rate among millennials is lower than prior generations, and student loan debt is a major contributing factor. Marriage is another life decision that tends to increase home ownership, and we have seen evidence suggesting[48] that student loan debt has contributed to young Americans' decisions to delay marriage.

In terms of retirement savings, Figure 2.11 shows how at every age from 25 to 35 among males, millennials in 2016 had a lower rate of participation in retirement plans than late baby boomers in 1989. At 35, 51 percent of male baby boomers had participated in a retirement plan, compared with just 37 percent of millennials—a reflection of the student loan burden as well as the fact that fewer jobs offer retirement plans as compared with previous decades. The numbers for female workers, shown in Figure 2.12, are not as drastic, due to the increasing number of women in the workforce over time, but the overall story is the same, with millennials participating at a lower rate.[49]

Other researchers at the center established that

Bachelor's degree-holders who have student loans have significantly lower retirement assets at age 30 than those without loans, indicating that having a student loan payment each month reduces retirement plan contribution rates.[50]

Interestingly, the study also determined

The actual size of the student loan does not seem to matter—those with student loans have lower retirement savings, but retirement wealth accumulation is similar for those with small loans and large loans.[51]

Specifically, college degree holders with student loans who participated in a retirement plan, had median retirement assets of $10,360 at age 30, compared with $18,270 for those without loans.[52]

Another way of looking at the effect of student loans on overall preparedness for retirement is through the National Retirement Risk Index, which estimates people's projected retirement income relative to their working-age income, and then compares that with the level they'd need to maintain their standards of living. Based on these calculations, Munnell and her colleagues concluded that 60.1 percent of households with student debt were considered "at risk," compared with 49.2 percent of those without such loans.[53]

Combine all the effects described in this chapter together,

FIGURE 2.11. PERCENTAGE OF MALE WORKERS PARTICIPATING IN AN EMPLOYER-SPONSORED RETIREMENT PLAN, AGES 25–35.

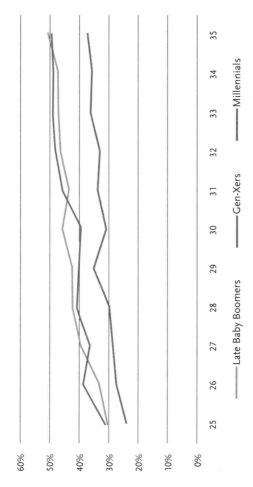

Source: Alice H. Munnell and Wenliang Hou, *Will Millennials Be Ready for Retirement?* (Boston, MA: Center for Retirement Research, 2018), Figure 6, https://crr.bc.edu/briefs/will-millennials-be-ready-for-retirement/.

Figure 2.12. Percentage of Female Workers Participating in an Employer-Sponsored Retirement Plan, Ages 25–35.

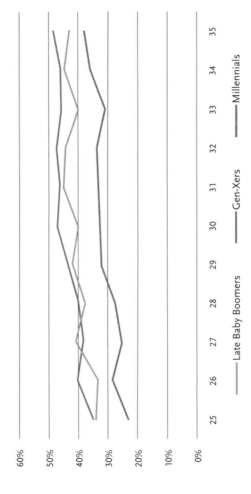

Source: Alice H. Munnell and Wenliang Hou, *Will Millennials Be Ready for Retirement?* (Boston, MA: Center for Retirement Research, 2018), Figure 6. https://crr.bc.edu/briefs/will-millennials-be-ready-for-retirement/.

and what we're seeing is a significant decline in overall net wealth among millennials as compared to previous generations at their same age. As Figure 2.13 shows, the net wealth-to-income ratio was noticeably higher for late baby boomers than it was for millennials at nearly every age between 20 and 34.[54]

A look at more recent Federal Reserve data shows how millennials are lagging behind their predecessors when it comes to building wealth. As shown in Figure 2.14, in 1989, households headed by individuals 35-and-under (i.e., late baby boomers) had an inflation-adjusted median net worth of $14,600. In 2016, millennials who were now in the same age group had a net worth of $11,000. That means the net worth of millennials is 25 percent lower than late boomers at the same age. In contrast, Figure 2.15 shows that current retirement age baby boomers are significantly better off than seniors were decades ago. Wealth for those aged 65 to 74 soared 56 percent, from an inflation-adjusted $143,100 in 1989 to $223,000 in 2016.[55]

The bottom line is that despite evidence of income rising in the past few years as the economy expanded, millennials are facing tremendous financial obstacles. They entered the workforce into a weaker economy. Living costs are higher than those faced by previous generations. And more than anything, the staggering growth in college costs has meant crushing debt that is not only squeezing them currently, but also making it harder to meet longer-term life goals including

FIGURE 2.13. WEALTH-TO-INCOME RATIO.

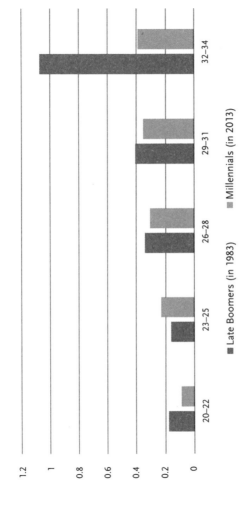

Source: Authors' calculations based on U.S. Board of Governors of the Federal Reserve System, Survey of Consumer Finances (SCF) (1983–2013).

* When using these data, please cite the Center for Retirement Research at Boston College.http://crr.bc.edu/wp-content/uploads/2016/01/IB_16-2.pdf.

getting married, purchasing a home, and saving for retirement. This leaves them ill-prepared for the massive storm ahead.

FIGURE 2.14. MEDIAN NET WORTH OF AMERICANS UNDER 35 (IN 2016 DOLLARS).

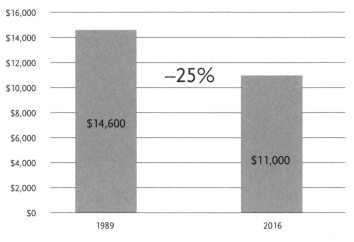

FIGURE 2.15. MEDIAN NET WORTH OF AMERICANS 65 AND OVER (IN 2016 DOLLARS).

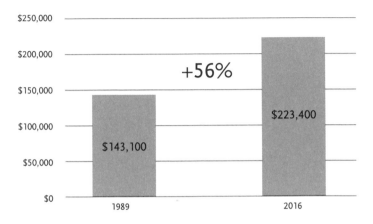

Source for Figures 2.14 and 2.15: "Survey of Consumer Finances (SCR):
Table 4," Board of Governors of the Federal Reserve System, last modified July 23, 2018,
https://www.federalreserve.gov/econres/scfindex.htm.

CHAPTER THREE

The Ghost of Millennials' Future

IN MAKING the pitch for Social Security personal investment accounts in his 2005 State of the Union speech,[1] former President George W. Bush declared that, absent action, "Thirteen years from now, in 2018, Social Security will be paying out more than it takes in . . . By the year 2042, the entire system would be exhausted and bankrupt."

At the time, his warnings were portrayed as alarmist. Democrats insisted that there was no crisis, Bush's political capital eroded, Republicans lost the nerve to act, and nothing was done to address the issue. We now know that the projections cited by Bush were indeed off—but only because they were overly optimistic. In reality, the Social Security system has been paying out more than it takes in through taxes since 2010. And that date Bush referred to way out in the future, when the system becomes exhausted, has since moved up seven years to 2035.[2] In other words, the day of reckoning that was 37 years into the future when Bush spoke about it is now just 16 years away.

Up to this point we have looked at how the debt inherited by millennials was significantly higher than the relatively modest debt inherited by baby boomers when they entered the workforce. We also saw how the tremendous growth in costs and precarious timing of when they entered into the workforce have punished the younger generation, limiting their ability to build wealth and prepare for retirement. Now it's time to take a deeper look at what the impact of this will be on millennials in the coming decades.

As we emphasized in Chapter 1, the idea of a Social Security "trust fund" is an accounting fiction, because current retirement benefits are funded by taxes and deficit spending rather than out of some mythical bank account. Nevertheless, the "trust fund" does have certain legal implications. Because baby boomers and the lawmakers they elected spent decades using surplus Social Security tax revenue to help subsidize other parts of the budget, the Social Security system built up a trust fund balance that requires the U.S. Treasury to keep paying full benefits to retirees even though there isn't enough dedicated tax revenue to support them. However, once that trust fund runs out, the U.S. government cannot legally pay more in benefits than it takes in with dedicated Social Security tax revenue. At that point, currently projected to come a decade and a half from now, payroll taxes would only be sufficient to pay 80 percent of scheduled benefits, meaning, absent action, retirees at that time would be facing the prospect of having their benefits slashed by 20 percent.[3]

In reality, lawmakers are unlikely to let retired baby boomers face that sort of immediate and drastic benefit cut. More likely is that the solution will be to increase payroll taxes or impose cuts on the working-age population, which at the time, would be primarily comprised of millennials who would be in their 30s, 40s, and 50s. And the increase in taxes could be substantial and would only grow the longer lawmakers wait to act.

But this is just one program. In addition to Social Security, the flood of baby boomers coupled with rising health care costs is going to lead to an explosion of spending on Medicare. Medicare is a more complicated program than Social Security in that it's divided into multiple parts, some of which are funded by payroll taxes like Social Security, but others are offset by revenue from premiums, which are subject to annual increases. The core Medicare program covering hospital stays, home health services, skilled nursing facilities, and hospice care has a trust fund like Social Security, only its trust fund is expected to be depleted even sooner—in 2026. At that point, existing taxes will only be able to cover 89 percent[4] of the costs of this part of Medicare, and by 2043 that number will drop to 78 percent.[5] This doesn't account for other costs of Medicare, including the parts that cover doctor visits and prescription drugs.

Adding up the combined long-term deficits of Social Security and Medicare produces numbers so absurdly large that it's difficult for most normal people to conceive of. Over the next 75 years, the present value of the combined gap between revenues and expected costs is a staggering $59 trillion.[6] That's just for these two programs that will primarily be benefitting baby boomers in the coming decades. According to CBO projections, the total federal debt is expected to reach $99.5 trillion by 2049, which is the end of its projection period.[7]

As shown in Figure 3.1, during the period that the first baby boomers were in the workforce (1946 to 2011), public debt averaged 36 percent of GDP. Now that millennials are in the workforce, it's more than double that amount. By the time early millennials approach retirement age in the 2040s, it will be four times the average debt burden experienced by baby boomers.

It should be noted that all these projections make certain assumptions about the economy, interest rates, tax revenue, and spending that could be way off, thus making the outlook significantly better or worse, depending in which direction CBO erred. In the unlikely scenario that lawmakers allow Social Security benefits to be cut dramatically for retirees once the trust fund becomes exhausted (in 2032, in CBO's estimate), then that would result in lower debt. This is the "payable-benefits scenario" in Figure 3.2. If interest rates are higher than expected, tax revenue is lower than anticipated, and spending is higher than expected, that 144 percent of GDP could turn into debt of 219 percent of GDP. That means that debt would be greater than two years of combined U.S. economic output.[8]

FIGURE 3.1. DEBT AS A PERCENTAGE OF GDP IN SELECTED YEARS.

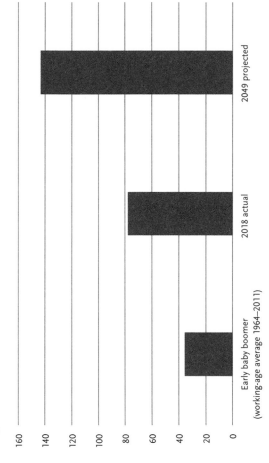

Sources: Years 1964–1968: Christine Bogusz, Leah Mazade, John Skeen, and Christian Spoor, eds., *The Budget and Economic Outlook: Fiscal Years 2004–2013*, (Washington, DC: Congressional Budget Office, 2003), Table F-1, 148, https://www.cbo.gov/sites/default/files /108th-congress-2003-2004/reports/entirereport_witherrata.pdf; Years 1969-2018: "Historical Budget Data, January 2019, Table 1." Congressional Budget Office, https://www.cbo.gov/about/products/budget-economic-data#2; Projection for 2049: "Long-Term Budget Projections, June 2019" Congressional Budget Office, https://www.cbo.gov/about/products/budget-economic-data#1.

What we've seen to this point is that unless projections are way off, our nation's debt is heading to unprecedented territory, and that's primarily the result of more spending on retiring baby boomers. What's scary is that the mix of tax increases and revenue cuts necessary to sustain debt even at its current historically elevated level of 78 percent of GDP is staggering, and it becomes even more daunting the longer lawmakers wait to act.[9]

Even if Congress were to magically address the problem in 2020, lawmakers would have to come up with a reduction in deficits of 1.8 percent of GDP—or about $400 billion based on today's GDP—every year going forward just to keep debt around where it is now in 2049. That's roughly the equivalent of eliminating Medicaid, or tripling the amount of corporate taxes collected. If Congress waits until 2030, that number would go up to 2.7 percent. That means within 10 years, Congress could eliminate the equivalent of the base defense budget each year, and it still wouldn't be enough to maintain long-term debt at its current elevated levels.[10] If lawmakers waited until 2030 and actually wanted to return debt to its average of the last 50 years,[11] that is, more in line with what the baby boomers experienced, it would require 4.4 percent of annual deficit reduction. That would translate into an across-the-board increase of income taxes by nearly 50 percent.[12]

Waiting longer to address the issue not only makes the math more daunting, it also ensures that millennials are

FIGURE 3.2. FEDERAL DEBT HELD BY THE PUBLIC.

Percentage of Gross Domestic Product, by Fiscal Year.

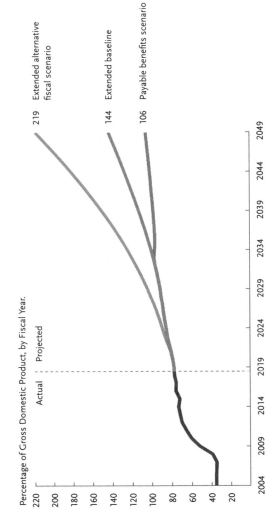

Source: "Long-Term Budget Projections, June 2019, Figure 2.1," Congressional Budget Office, https://www.cbo.gov/about/products/budget-economic-data#1.

going to disproportionately absorb the burden of any changes, while it increases the likelihood that baby boomers will skate by without having to pay the piper. That is, right now, there are still baby boomers in the workforce who are paying taxes and who could be affected by any changes to the Social Security and Medicare systems. As they age out of the workforce, they will be less and less affected by any increase in taxes. At the same time, most proposals to reform retirement programs typically aim to exempt (or at least limit) the effects of any changes to current retirees. This stems from the understandable sentiment that those currently retired built their lives around the existing system and once in retirement have a much more limited ability to adjust to any changes. In practice, this deference means that the longer lawmakers wait to act, the more baby boomers will retire and be "grandfathered in" to the old unsustainable system, shielding them from any reforms that could reduce benefits for the retirees who come after them.

Just to illustrate, by 2029, the last baby boomers will have reached retirement age. Meanwhile, millennials in their 30s and 40s will be in their prime working years. If nothing is done until then, that means that baby boomers will have left behind a giant mountain of debt, without having had to pay higher taxes or sacrifice any of their promised retirement benefits. In contrast, millennials will almost certainly have to pay substantially higher taxes to make sure the boomers get paid, and yet despite contributing more, are unlikely to get the benefits they have been promised.

But focusing on the magnitude of spending cuts or tax increases that would be required to constrain the overwhelming increase in federal debt in the coming decades does not account for how hamstrung federal policymakers would be in trying to address other national priorities, or in responding to unexpected national emergencies, such as severe economic downturns or security threats.

In 1932, when Franklin Delano Roosevelt was elected president, and just before the New Deal was launched in response to the Great Depression, federal spending was the equivalent of 6.8 percent of GDP. That left policymakers significant fiscal room to respond to the twin events of the economic collapse, and then, World War II.[13] In 2019, Social Security, Medicare and interest payments alone account for 9.7 percent of GDP, and as we have seen, they are growing significantly, and total federal spending is eventually projected to approach 30 percent of GDP. With the nation drowning in debt even without authorizing any new spending, policymakers will be in no position to respond to the unexpected.

While baby boomers grew up with the United States as a superpower, and hit middle age when the Soviet Union collapsed, in the coming decades, millennials will have more constraints in responding to international challenges. As we have seen, U.S. military spending is getting increasingly crowded out by spending on retirees. By 2021, U.S. defense spending is projected to drop to 2.8 percent of GDP, which is the lowest level since 1940—and then continue down from there, reaching 2.5 percent by the end of the coming decade. That's less than half the 5.1 percent of GDP that the United States spent on defense, on average, during the working-age years of the first baby boomers (1964–2011). Sure, it could be argued that as the world's most powerful military, there's room to downsize. But how will there be room to grow in the future if necessary?[14]

It has become popular for politicians to lament the crumbling infrastructure in the United States and long for the days when the United States was able to engage in massive building projects. "America is the nation that built the transcontinental railroad, brought electricity to rural communities, constructed the Interstate Highway System," President Obama reminded us in his 2011 State of the Union Address, before ending the speech with the call to action, "We do big things."[15]

It was fitting that Obama made the speech in the same year that the first wave of baby boomers began to retire, because if anybody is looking for a reason why America can no longer do "big things," they need look no farther than the amount of spending that has already been committed to retirees.

When legislation was passed in 1956 creating the interstate highway system, just 8 percent of noninterest spending went to finance Social Security, and Medicare didn't exist yet. As we've seen, those two programs currently absorb about 40 percent of the budget today—a number that is growing each year. In 2049, by the time the federal government pays Social Security and Medicare benefits and meets its interest obligations, 92 percent of expected revenue will have been eaten up[16] before a penny is spent on defense, education, Medicaid, Obamacare, anti-poverty programs, infrastructure, or any other national priority.

Millennials, however, may not have decades to wait. There's a growing chance that well before debt reaches this point, the nation will face what economists refer to as a "fiscal crisis" in which investors lose faith in the United States, and wince at extending the nation more credit, leading to a vicious circle that's difficult to get out of. The possibility of a fiscal crisis is the subject of a lot of debate within the economics profession, and there's no magic formula to predict when it might happen, or exactly how it could come about. But it's widely believed that at the minimum, massive and growing debt without any response from lawmakers makes such a crisis significantly more likely.

"A large and continuously growing federal debt would increase the chance of a fiscal crisis in the United States," Keith Hall, then director of the CBO, said in response to written questions from the Senate Budget Committee in 2017.[17]

He expanded

Specifically, investors might become less willing to finance federal borrowing unless they were compensated with high returns. If so, interest rates on federal debt would rise abruptly, dramatically increasing the cost of government borrowing. That increase would reduce the market value of outstanding government securities, and investors could lose money. The resulting losses for mutual funds, pension funds, insurance companies, banks, and other holders of government debt might be large enough to cause some financial institutions to fail, creating a fiscal crisis. An additional result would be a higher cost for private-sector borrowing because uncertainty about the government's responses could reduce confidence in the viability of private-sector enterprises. . . . It is impossible for anyone to accurately predict whether or when such a fiscal crisis might occur in the United States. In particular, the debt-to-GDP ratio has no identifiable tipping point to indicate that a crisis is likely or imminent. All else being equal, however, the larger a government's debt, the greater the risk of a fiscal crisis.[18]

Hall explained that if the United States got to this point, lawmakers would be forced to choose among only bad options.

If a fiscal crisis occurred in the United States, policymakers would have only limited—and unattractive—options for responding. The government

would need to undertake some combination of
three approaches: restructure the debt (that is, seek
to modify the contractual terms of existing obligations), use monetary policy to raise inflation above
expectations, or adopt large and abrupt spending
cuts or tax increases.[19]

In other words, either millennials would have to face dramatic cuts to government services, fork over substantially
more in taxes just to mollify creditors, or face hyperinflation,
which will increase the cost of everything and thus significantly reduce their purchasing power.

All of these options, however, just create more problems. Sudden and severe cuts to government spending or
increases in taxes, for instance, would disrupt people's lives
and cripple economic growth. When economic growth stalls
and people lose jobs or face salary cuts, government revenue falls while dependence on social safety net programs
increases, which exacerbates deficits—undercutting auster-
ity policies. Printing more money and paying back creditors
with devalued currency is a form of default, making it more
likely that investors would demand ever higher interest rates,
which would mean the federal government would have to
devote even more to borrowing costs, putting even more of
a squeeze on the rest of the budget.

In 2018, Deutsche Bank economists Quinn Brody and
Torsten Slok wrote a research note titled, "A coming debt

crisis in the US?"[20] Based on an economic model, they determined that the threat of a fiscal crisis in the United States
was relatively small, but that it was growing. Specifically,
they found, "the deteriorating fiscal and external situation
for the United States have increased the probability of a US
debt crisis by 7 percentage points, from a historical average
below 9 [percent] to a level around 16 [percent]."

The economists noted that because the dollar is a reserve
currency and the United States borrows in its own currency,
there is likely no "immediate risk" of such a crisis, but they
pointed to several ominous trends. One is that, according to
the International Monetary Fund (IMF), the United States is
the only country that is expected to see its debt-to-GDP ratio
grow over the next five years. Another is evidence of soften-
ing foreign demand for U.S. debt even as the supply of debt
is rising. The other came from looking at the relationship
between the unemployment rate and deficits going back to
1949, data that is reproduced here in Figure 3.3.

What they observed was that typically the government
runs larger deficits during recessions while those deficits tend
to shrink when the economy is booming. This makes sense—
in a slowing economy, so-called "automatic stabilizers" kick
in to help cushion the blow and more people become dependent on programs such as food stamps and unemployment
insurance. At the same time, with more people out of work
and incomes falling, tax revenue tends to fall. The reverse is
true during a booming economy, as tax collections tend to

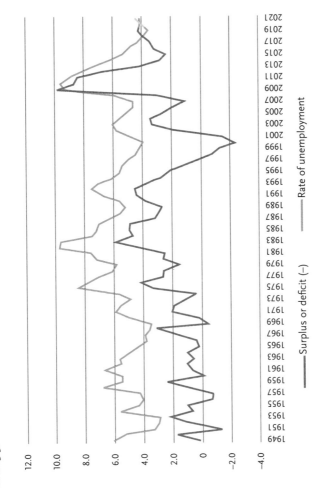

FIGURE 3.3. DEFICITS ARE EXPANDING EVEN AS UNEMPLOYMENT RATE PLUMMETS.

Sources: "Historical Tables, Table 1.2–Summary of Receipts, Outlays, and Surpluses or Deficits (-) as Percentages of GDP: 1930–2024,"
White House Office of Management and Budget, https://www.whitehouse.gov/omb/historical-tables/; "Labor Force Statistics from the
Current Population Survey: Unemployment Rate" Bureau of Labor Statistics, https://data.bls.gov/timeseries/LNS14000000.

rise and people enter the workforce and become less dependent on the safety net. Yet right now, we're seeing a break from this trend as deficits are increasing even as the economy is experiencing the lowest unemployment rate in nearly 50 years.

Brody and Slok note that thus far interest rates have remained low as the United States is still seen as a good risk for investors looking for somewhere safe to park their money. "Eventually, however this will become unsustainable," they conclude. "We cannot say exactly what level of debt (85 [percent] of GDP? 100 [percent]? 125 [percent]?) will prove to be the tipping point, but we do believe that the latest fiscal developments have increased the odds of a crisis."[21]

Millennials, thus, are facing grim prospects. They entered the workforce encumbered with debt and have had difficulty building up wealth and preparing for retirement. But the mounting federal debt will force them to make difficult choices never faced by any previous generation, between paying significantly higher taxes to support baby boomers and/or accepting significantly fewer government benefits. Waiting longer to act will only make the choices more severe, and ignoring the problem entirely will greatly increase the risks of a fiscal crisis and all of the crushing economic consequences that come along with it.

CHAPTER FOUR

The Anti-Youth Lobby

≥≤

IN DECEMBER 2012, former Wyoming Sen. Alan Simpson, who had just cochaired a bipartisan deficit reduction panel, became an Internet sensation. The octogenarian starred in a YouTube video[1] that featured him awkwardly dancing next to a giant soda can[2] to the tune of the viral South Korean pop song "Gangnam Style." The gag was an effort to draw attention to the group "The Can Kicks Back," an organization that had launched the previous month with a goal of mobilizing millennials to demand action on the federal debt.[3] As part of the effort, the group rallied Congress, published op-eds, issued reports, and toured college campuses to raise awareness of the debt issue, and the threat it posed to the younger generation in particular. The giant soda can dancing next to Simpson actually had a name—"AmeriCAN"—and served as the group's mascot.

"Our generation is the can that politicians keep kicking down the road," the group's cofounder, Nick Troiano, said when the group launched. "This campaign is an opportunity for young Americans to finally kick back at Washington and demand a solution to our country's $16 trillion and growing national debt."[4] By February 2014, or less than a year and a half later, Politico reported that the group was running out of money[5] and it soon fizzled. Try to visit its website now, and it redirects to a page that reads, "Hi There! Were you looking for The Can Kicks Back? Fortunately, The Can Kicks Back no longer exists." The defunct organization's domain name had been bought out by Social Security Works, an activist group that perpetuates the idea that there's no Social Security crisis, and instead argues that the program needs to be dramatically expanded.[6]

The demise of The Can Kicks Back, one of many failed efforts to draw attention to the burden being placed on millennials, is representative of the uphill battle faced by fiscal realists in the face of powerful special interest groups that have billions of dollars riding on the status quo. Baby boomers flex their political muscles to make sure no major changes are made to retirement programs. Meanwhile, there's no countervailing force pressuring lawmakers to make substantial reforms to put the nation's debt on a sustainable course. Sure, there are groups such as the Committee for a Responsible Federal Budget or the Peter G. Peterson Foundation, as well as plenty of think tankers and columnists railing against the rising debt, but that is separate from actual effective political activism that makes lawmakers fear losing their jobs if they refuse to tackle the debt. As a result, politicians have much to risk by tackling the problem, while they have little to gain. So they choose the path of least resistance and do nothing.

Lack of action on the debt is not confined to any particular party. The federal debt has mounted for decades, with Republican and Democratic presidents and alternating party control of Congress. In 2009, former President Obama's first budget was named, "A New Era of Fiscal Responsibility,"[7] yet by the time he left office he had overseen a doubling of the national debt. Former House Speaker Paul Ryan rose to political stardom for championing a bold plan to overhaul the nation's entitlement programs. But he retired from two decades in the House with a record only of having expanded entitlement programs and increased defense spending while voting to cut taxes without offsetting spending reductions.[8] He also negotiated deals allowing Congress to bust through caps that had been put in place as part of a 2011 compromise to modestly restrain spending. As a new election year approaches, Republicans are led by the populist President Trump, who has eschewed the idea of reforming Medicare and Social Security, while Democrats seeking to replace him in the Oval Office have proposed tens of trillions of dollars of new spending.

In previous chapters, we have outlined why the growing national debt will be placing a heavy burden on millennials, who are already in a precarious financial position. Now it's worth delving a little deeper into why the problem is so hard to do anything about.

Any discussion about the politics of Social Security and Medicare requires a deeper look at the inner workings of AARP, the center of the anti-youth lobby. The group, often thought of as a harmless club through which older Americans enjoy discounted hotels and car rentals, is actually more of a massive insurance business and lobbying group. The group generates most of its revenues from royalties it receives from lending out its name to other companies selling products to its members. The bulk of the royalty income comes from United Health Group,[9] the nation's largest insurer, which sells AARP-branded policies to seniors that fill in the gaps in traditional Medicare coverage. These policies are often referred to as Medigap plans.

AARP's royalty income has enjoyed tremendous growth in recent decades as government has expanded. As shown in Figure 4.1, in 1999, royalty income was about $200 million, but by 2017, it had topped $909 million—an increase of over 350 percent. That growth came at a much faster clip than growth in membership income. In 2002, the two main sources of income were nearly comparable, with membership dues accounting for $186.3 million[10] in revenue and royalties bringing in $240 million. In 2017, royalties were more than triple the $301 million generated from membership dues.

Overall, in 2017, as seen in Figure 4.2, 55 percent of AARP's total revenue came from royalties, compared with just 18 percent that came from membership. The organization

FIGURE 4.1. AARP's GROWING EMPIRE.

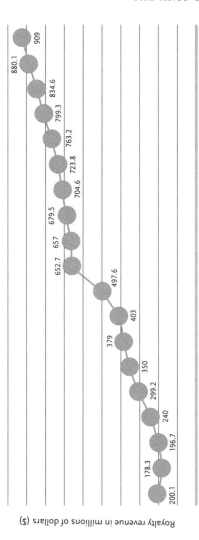

Royalty revenue in millions of dollars ($)

200.1 178.3 196.7 240 299.2 350 379 403 497.6 652.7 657 679.5 704.6 723.8 763.2 799.3 834.6 880.1 909

1999 2000 2001 2002 2003 2004 2005 2006 2007 2008 2009 2010 2011 2012 2013 2014 2015 2016 2017

Sources: For 1999–2008: Thomas C. Nelson, "Nov. 2, 2009 Correspondence to David G Reichert," AARP, https://www.aarp.org/about-aarp/info-03-2011/november_reichert_nelson.html; For 2009–2017: AARP Consolidated Financial Statements December 31, 2009 and 2008, published March 24, 2010, https://assets.aarp.org/www.aarp.org-/cs/misc/2009_aarp_consolidated_financial_statements_12-31_09.pdf; AARP Consolidated Financial Statements December 31, 2011 and 2010, published March 23, 2012, https://www.aarp.org/content/dam/aarp/about_aarp/annual_reports/2012-05/Consolidated-Financial-Statements-2011-2010-AARP.pdf; Consolidated Financial Statements Together with Report of Independent Certified Public Accountants AARP December 31, 2013 and 2012, published March 26, 2014, https://www.aarp.org/content/dam/aarp/about_aarp/annual_reports/2014-06/2013-Consolidated-Financial-Statements-AARP.pdf; Consolidated Financial Statements Together with Report of Independent Certified Public Accountants AARP December 31, 2015 and 2014, published March 17, 2016, https://www.aarp.org/content/dam/aarp/about_aarp/annual_reports/2016/2015-financial-statements-AARP.pdf; Consolidated Financial Statements Together with Report of Independent Certified Public Accountants AARP December 31, 2017 and 2016, published March 16, 2018, https://www.aarp.org/content/dam/aarp/about_aarp/about_us/2018/aarp-2017-audited-financial-statement.pdf.

generated a total of $1.6 billion in revenue that year from all sources.

All of the money flowing into AARP each year helps fuel its massive lobbying operation, through which it promotes policies that expand government, prevent any real reforms to entitlements, and exacerbate the long-term debt problem. Conveniently, the changes AARP advocates tend to further boost its bottom line.

FIGURE 4.2. ROYALTIES MAKE UP THE MAJORITY OF AARP's $1.6 BILLION REVENUE.

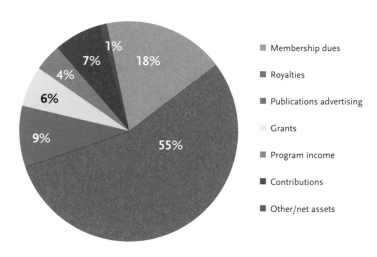

Source: *Consolidated Financial Statements Together with Report of Independent Certified Public Accountants AARP December 31, 2017 and 2016*, published March 16, 2018, https://www.aarp.org /content/dam/aarp/about_aarp/about_us/2018/aarp-2017-audited-financial-statement.pdf

As shown in Table 4.1, AARP was cumulatively the ninth largest lobbying group over the two decades from 1998 to 2018. During that period, it spent more on lobbying than major defense contractors (Boeing, Northrop Grumman, Lockheed Martin), the biggest oil company (ExxonMobil), and the biggest telecommunications companies (AT&T, Verizon, and Comcast).

TABLE 4.1. CUMULTAIVE LOBBYING SPENDING 1998–2018.	
GROUP	SPENT LOBBYING
US Chamber of Commerce	$1,506,125,680
National Assn of Realtors	$543,448,083
American Medical Assn	$393,194,500
American Hospital Assn	$372,445,855
PhRMA	$364,374,550
General Electric	$359,612,000
Blue Cross/Blue Shield	$347,554,491
Business Roundtable	$284,120,000
AARP	**$282,621,064**
Boeing Co	$274,803,310
Northrop Grumman	$272,125,213

Table continues on next page

Group	Spent lobbying
Lockheed Martin	$255,304,170
Exxon Mobil	$254,742,742
AT&T Inc	$248,514,644
Verizon Communications	$244,959,109
National Assn of Broadcasters	$229,248,000
Edison Electric Institute	$224,795,955
Southern Co	$223,210,694
Altria Group	$197,775,200
Comcast Corp	$197,534,323

Source: Center for Responsive Politics.

As Figure 4.3 shows, however, AARP lobbying spending spikes when its core issues are being debated. Lobbying soared during 2003 when the Medicare prescription drug plan was being debated and in 2005 when President Bush called for Social Security personal accounts. It remained elevated in 2008 through 2011, as Congress contemplated changes to Medicare, Obamacare passed into law, and various ideas were being floated to reform entitlements. During the years 2003, 2005, and 2008 AARP was actually the second-highest ranking lobbyist, behind only the U.S. Chamber of Commerce.[11]

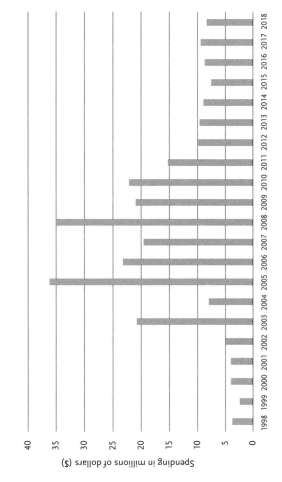

FIGURE 4.3. ANNUAL AARP LOBBYING.

Source: "AARP Client Profile: Summary, 2018," Center for Responsive Politics lobbying database, https://www.opensecrets.org/lobby/clientsum.php?id=D000023726&year=2018.

Looking purely at money being spent, however, understates the group's influence, which is boosted by the fact that it can claim 38 million members.[12] AARP changed its name from the American Association of Retired Persons to reflect the fact that since 1984, it has been open to Americans who reach the age of 50, and thus many of its members are still in the workforce. There are now 114 million[13] Americans 50 or over, meaning roughly a third of them are AARP members.

More politically significant is that this is also a massive and active voting bloc. In the 2018 midterm elections, 56 percent of voters were 50 or over.[14] So when AARP lobbies members of Congress, it doesn't only have the ability to spend money, it also carries the implicit threat of being able to sic tens of millions of retirees on lawmakers—a politically engaged group with plenty of time on their hands. "I was a United States Senator since I was 29 years old, my experience is I've never lost with the AARP behind me," Joe Biden said in 2009.[15]

Most of the time AARP's lobbying positions are predictable—fighting for expansion of retirement benefits and against any effort to rein them in. For instance, the organization supported Bush's effort to expand Medicare to cover prescription drugs,[16] but opposed his subsequent effort to reform Social Security.[17] During the Obama years, it opposed Ryan's budgets that would have overhauled Medicare,[18] but also protested more modest bipartisan proposals to slow the rate of growth of Social Security by tying benefits to a different measure of inflation.[19]

In its support for the passage of Obamacare, however, we saw what happened when the desires of its membership conflicted with its ideological leanings and business interests. Among its many other provisions, Obamacare included over $700 billion in cuts to projected Medicare spending.[20] Instead of being used to shore up Medicare's finances, that money was used to help finance the creation of the new health care entitlement.

On the surface, it would seem this was a bill that AARP would have opposed, especially given that its core membership was more vociferously opposed to the bill than any other group. A September 2009 Gallup survey taken when Obamacare was making its way through Congress found that just 32 percent of those 65 years and older supported the bill, compared with 42 percent who opposed it—a wider margin of opposition than all other age groups polled.[21]

In reality, however, AARP was a significant booster of Obamacare, even hosting several events with Obama[22] and other administration officials to make the case for the legislation. How to explain the seeming contradiction? It turns out that the new law was designed in a way that boosted demand for AARP insurance products. At the same time, AARP was able to fend off any changes to Medigap regulations that would have hindered its business, and made sure those policies were exempt from many of Obamacare's mandates that affected other types of insurance.[23]

Although AARP is a major obstacle to reform, the group is by no means the only powerful lobbying group with an interest in preserving or building on the status quo. With a budget set to exceed $1 trillion[24] in the coming years, Medicare is a massive honey pot for the health insurance industry, and the major players act accordingly.

In 2003, PhRMA lobbied heavily for the passage of the Medicare prescription drug program, which meant hundreds of billions of dollars flowing into the drug industry.[25] The same bill included provisions that meant more money for hospitals.[26] To this day, hospitals lobby against any reforms to Medicare that would limit the payments they receive from the program.

In 1997, Congress and President Clinton struck a bipartisan deal to control the rate of growth of doctors' payments within Medicare. When push came to shove, however, amid outcry from the American Medical Association, Congress repeatedly voted to avoid the cuts, a policy that became known as the "doc fix." In 2015, the AMA successfully lobbied to end the charade and permanently do away with the scheduled cuts - a rare bipartisan agreement between Obama and the Republican Congress.[27]

The bigger Medicare gets, the more baby boomers it covers, the harder it is to make changes. Policymakers who want to make changes have to deal not only with AARP, which will rally against any real reforms, but also with the massive publicly traded corporations that have billions of dollars in profits tied to the program.

One could write a separate book focusing exclusively on the historical politics surrounding the federal debt. Such an exhaustive history is beyond the scope of our current discussion, but it is important to dip in so as to recognize how we got to the current place in time, in which debt is exploding but both parties are more determined than ever to ignore it.

The federal debt problem, it should be noted, is not the province of any one party. Since World War II, deficits have averaged 2.3 percent while Republican presidents have been in power and 2 percent when Democratic presidents have been in office, with control of Congress varying.[28] Both parties have played a role in creating and preserving the status quo.

Ronald Reagan, despite being the symbol of the resurgence of limited-government beliefs in America, actually helped enshrine a politically successful but ultimately destructive fiscal management strategy that dominates Republican thinking to this day. To be sure, it should be stipulated that Reagan had a Democratic House for his full two terms in office. And in 1983, he embraced bipartisan changes recommended by the Greenspan Commission that dealt with a Social Security financing issue. It led to reforms that included a mix of payroll tax increases and benefit changes (such as gradually increasing the retirement age to

67 by 2027). But at the same time, Reagan's famous sunny optimism fed into the baby boomer mentality of instant gratification—the idea that we can have everything we want without tradeoffs. During his two terms, he combined tax cuts with significant increases in defense spending, without real efforts to rein in entitlement spending. This served as the fiscal model for the subsequent Republican presidencies of George W. Bush and Trump, both of whom also combined tax cuts with increases in military spending without longer-term debt reduction. In Bush's case, he pushed through the largest expansion of entitlements since the Great Society in the form of the Medicare prescription drug plan, which was not paid for.

One reason that the Reagan approach survives to this day is not only because of his political successes, but also due to the failure of George H.W. Bush when he deviated from the model. Six words were essential to the legacy of Bush and crucial to understanding the political dynamics surrounding the current debt debate: "Read my lips: no new taxes."[29] When Bush broke that campaign promise as part of a 1990 budget deal, it created a significant backlash from conservatives that helped fuel Pat Buchanan's primary challenge and later helped Bill Clinton muddy the waters on the issue of honesty during the 1992 election. On top of that, what became clear within a few years was that while taxes did indeed increase as a result of the deal, the proposed spending cuts did not go through. To the extent there were spending cuts, they came on the defense side of the ledger, which largely had to do with the downsizing of the military at the end of the Cold War.[30]

Future Republican officeholders took a key lesson from the Bush legacy as it related to fiscal policy: Never trade tax increases for promised spending cuts, because the spending cuts will never go through and the tax hikes will cost you re-election. From then on, Republicans have largely remained loyal to the anti-tax pledges they signed, with Grover Norquist's Americans for Tax Reform working tirelessly to hold them to their promises.

If you want to know why Republicans were unwilling to sign on to any sort of bipartisan deficit reduction deal with Obama, look no further than the contrast between the political success of Reagan and the failure of the elder Bush.

Democrats have seen themselves as the stewards of the massive entitlement state that was put into motion by Democratic presidents, mainly by Franklin Roosevelt and Lyndon B. Johnson, with additional expansions by Clinton and Obama. At every turn, Democrats have always used the prospect of Republicans going after seniors as a central part of their campaign strategy, an attack that Republicans have sought to diffuse by acceding to the growing welfare state.

Back in 1980, Reagan's famous "There you go again" quip was actually in response to Jimmy Carter attacking Reagan over his opposition to the version of Medicare that passed in 1965. Reagan responded that he had preferred an alternate proposal, but had not objected to the overall concept.[31]

In 1995, when a new Republican-led Congress vowed to reduce projected Medicare spending by 14 percent over seven years, Clinton warned their proposed cuts would have "draconian consequences" and would "dismantle Medicare as we know it."[32]

In 2005, when Bush proposed to reform Social Security, rather than promoting an alternative, Democrats settled on a different strategy: simply deny there was a crisis. "If we let the president successfully convince people there's a crisis in Social Security, when in fact there is no crisis at all, then shame on us," former Sen. Byron Dorgan of North Dakota said, who at the time was chairman of the Senate Democratic Policy Committee.[33] The next year, Democrats won back control of Congress, in no small part due to their successful campaign against Bush's proposed changes to Social Security.

In 2011, when Republicans took back the House and Paul Ryan, who had made a name in the minority for authoring a sweeping plan to overhaul the nation's entitlements, became chairman of the Budget Committee, Democrats immediately attacked. Then Senate Majority Leader Harry Reid hosted a "Back off Social Security" rally with activists.[34] "It is not in crisis at this stage," he told MSNBC. "Leave Social Security alone. We have a lot of other places we can look that [are] in crisis. But Social Security is not." The 71-year-old Reid added: "Two decades from now, I'm willing to take a look at it. But I'm not willing to take a look at it right now."[35]

When Ryan unveiled the Republican budget, it didn't make changes to Social Security, but it did slowly transition Medicare from a one-sized-fits-all system to one in which seniors could choose among competing private plans whose premiums would be subsidized by the federal government. This would have injected more choice and competition into the system and allowed lawmakers to set the subsidies to grow at a sustainable rate.

"Medicare is a core value of our social compact with the American people, yet this budget shreds that contract, which is part of the strength of our country," Democratic leader Rep. Nancy Pelosi thundered on the House floor. "The Republican proposal breaks the promise that our country has made to our seniors, that after a lifetime of work they will be able to depend on Medicare to protect them in retirement. This plan, the Republican plan, ends Medicare as we know it and dramatically reduces benefits for seniors."[36]

An outside group, the Agenda Project, released an ad featuring a Paul Ryan look-alike rolling an elderly woman in a wheelchair down a path and then actually pushing the granny off of a cliff.[37]

Republicans are not immune to using such scare tactics, either. Among the most frequent attacks leveled against Obamacare by Republicans was that it slashed $716 billion from Medicare. An attack ad from the Mitt Romney-Paul

Ryan 2012 campaign even perpetuated the accounting fiction that the money being cut by Obamacare represented money that seniors had "paid into Medicare for years."[38] More recently, Republicans have responded to some Democrats rallying around socialized health insurance proposals that would transition everybody to a new government-run plan as the "end of Medicare as we know it" and as "a socialist experiment with Medicare."[39] It's odd to attack an expansion of government-run health care by arguing it would threaten government-run health care, but such is the protective bubble that both parties have put around the program.

Even as the debt problem has grown, in the past decade, politicians have expressed even less willingness to do something about it. A decade ago both parties agreed the debt was a significant problem, but just blamed the other party for its existence. These days, the parties don't even bother going through the charade.

Shortly after signing his $831 billion[40] economic stimulus bill into law in 2009, Obama convened a "fiscal responsibility summit" at the White House. He said

> We cannot, and will not, sustain deficits like these without end. Contrary to the prevailing wisdom in Washington these past few years, we cannot simply spend as we please and defer the consequences to the next budget, the next administration, or the next generation.[41]

From 2009 to 2012, however, Obama ran up deficits that exceeded $1 trillion each year, and on the day he left office, the debt was more than double what it was when he was sworn in.[42]

During the first term of the Obama administration, Republicans newly discovered an interest in tackling the debt that had gone into hibernation during the Bush years. On the Right, the Tea Party movement sprang up demanding a stricter adherence to the Constitution and a return to limited government. The Tea Party, in spite of its excesses, actually represented a potentially historic development in the politics of the debt. For the first time, members of Congress could actually fear primary challenges for voting to increase the debt or against efforts to tackle spending. This had the potential to upset the traditional dynamic in politics in which the path of least resistance was always to do nothing and allow spending to balloon. It led Republicans to embrace the Ryan plan to overhaul Medicare, and his plan even helped catapult him to a place on the 2012 ticket, and eventually, to Speaker of the House. It triggered a fight over raising the debt ceiling in 2011 that led to a deal which carried the promise of reducing deficits of $2.4 trillion.[43]

Ultimately, this proved short-lived. The movement lost steam over time and in 2016, gave way to Trumpism. Though Trump boasted in absurd terms about eliminating the debt within eight years while running for president,[44] he has ultimately represented a movement away from the Tea

Party and toward a new populism. He has pushed for cutting taxes, increasing military spending, and even spending more money on infrastructure. Significantly, instead of embracing Ryan-style entitlement reform, he has run away from it—vowing not to overhaul Medicare or Social Security.

Much of this was no doubt based on Trump's political instincts that entitlement reform was bad politics. But there are also data pointing to a structural problem that makes it difficult for Republicans to actually fight for entitlement reform. The reality is that older voters are the core part of the Republican constituency.

In 2016, exit polls showed that Hillary Clinton dominated Donald Trump among 18 to 44 year olds, 53 percent to 39 percent. But Trump bested her among those 45 and older by 52 percent to 44 percent—and the older bloc represented 56 percent of voters.[45] The generational divide had an even greater impact in the battleground states that ultimately delivered victory to Trump, including Michigan,[46] Wisconsin,[47] Ohio,[48] Pennsylvania,[49] and Florida.[50] In all those states, the proportion of older voters was higher than the national average. In Florida, where more than one-in-five voters is 65 or over, Trump dominated that group by 17 points.

So this gets at the crux of the issue. Millennials, who are most affected by the failure to address entitlements for older Americans, overwhelmingly back the Democratic Party, which is the party that created the programs and is traditionally positioned as their guardians. Meanwhile, though

Republicans on the surface are the party more resistant to the entitlement state, in actuality, they find it politically difficult to follow through on any actual reforms because they have become so dependent on older voters. And now, they aren't even pretending.

During the Trump administration, Republicans have abandoned all pretense of caring about the debt. They passed a $1.5 trillion tax cut[51] that was not offset by any sort of reductions in spending. They also blew up various spending restraints that were put in place by the 2011 debt ceiling deal that was the crowning achievement of the Tea Party so they could bolster the defense budget.[52] They have also, quite comfortably, acquiesced to Trump's unwillingness to address the twin Medicare and Social Security crises.

In March 2019, Trump released a budget that the White House touted as reducing deficits by $2.8 trillion over a decade. Eyebrows were immediately raised by a line item that suggested that Trump was cutting $845 billion from Medicare. But a closer look found that this was an illusion.

In fact, much of the deficit reduction came from making optimistic assumptions about economic growth. The Medicare "cuts," which triggered predictable attacks from Democrats, represented the classic Washington promise to reduce "waste, fraud, and abuse," and as the administration made clear, there were no plans for structural changes to any retirement programs. Acting OMB director Russ Vought said

He's not cutting Medicare in this budget. What we are doing is putting forward reforms that lower drug prices that because Medicare pays a very large share of drug prices in this country, has the impact of finding savings. We're also finding waste, fraud, and abuse, but Medicare spending will go up every single year by healthy margins and there are no structural changes for Medicare beneficiaries.[53]

A further analysis from the Committee for a Responsible Federal Budget found that up to 39 percent of the proposed Medicare savings represented spending that was simply reassigned to other parts of the budget, and the remaining $515 billion[54] of "cuts" were mainly repackaged tweaks to how Medicare pays for services that mostly built off of prior Obama proposals that at the time were rightly deemed insufficient by Republicans.

The experience of the past decade has also left Democrats more resistant to talk of debt reduction. At the time, Obama's nods toward debt reduction were taken by Republicans as an insincere effort to trick them into hiking taxes, but many liberals criticized him for even engaging on the issue. The fact that Republicans abandoned their grave concerns about the debt as soon as they regained control of the White House only bolstered the view that those concerns were phony.

Democrats are incensed that after years of obstructing

Obama's agenda with lectures on the unsustainable debt, after Trump took office with an improving economy, Republicans abandoned their concerns about spending while cutting taxes by $1.5 trillion. Leading candidates for the 2020 nomination are now using the 2017 tax cut as a justification for getting behind tens of trillions of dollars in sweeping new spending proposals without feeling the need to explain how they would pay for them. The prevailing view among liberals now is that it would be unilateral disarmament for Democrats to curb their ambitions in the face of outcries about the debt. So it's full speed ahead.

CHAPTER 5

The Socialism Trap

≥<

THESE DAYS, Sen. Bernie Sanders, I-VT, is the American politician most identified with the far-Left. But back during the 2004 election, that was Howard Dean. The former Vermont governor stormed to the lead[1] of the Democratic primary at one point by channeling all of the anger toward George W. Bush and finding a way to harness it through online activism. Like Sanders, he gained a passionate following and drew the ire of the party establishment. Yet by the standards of today's Democratic party, he was a right-winger.[2]

Dean actually described himself as "fiscally conservative"[3] throughout his ultimately unsuccessful campaign. In a January 2004 debate ahead of the Iowa caucuses, he complained, "If we don't balance the budget in this country, we're not going to have jobs. We're not going to have prosperity. You cannot promise people tax cuts, college education, health care and whatever else you want and say, 'Oh, it'll all be fine.'"[4]

It's hard to think of a statement that could be more

incongruous with the predominant thinking of today's liberal Democrats. In their view, excessive concern for fiscal restraint deepened the Great Recession, and should not be cited as an excuse for preventing the dramatic expansion of the social welfare state. In the 2020 campaign, Democratic presidential candidates have embraced ideas including a universal basic income, a federal government job guarantee, free college, universal child care, affordable housing, cancellation of student debt, and free health care for everybody. Even if these programs are too radical to happen in the near term, they are undeniably much more mainstream then they would have been just a few years ago, and a signal of where things could be heading as a new generation takes over the party.

Meanwhile, the idea that things will "be fine" if leaders dismiss questions about how to pay for ambitious proposals is actually an explicit position among a new crop of liberal economists.

Modern Monetary Theory (MMT) started as a fringe movement rejected by most economists, but it has gained notoriety in recent years as liberals have become frustrated with financial barriers to their agenda. The complex theory can be described in shorthand as the belief that a government that issues its own currency, such as the United States, could never actually face a debt crisis because it could always print more money to pay off debt and purchase whatever goods it wants.

Among many other issues, embracing MMT carries a significant risk of inflation, and the belief that Congress could always raise taxes in response to such a threat does not adequately account for the difficulty of passing such legislation before it's too late. Even liberal Paul Krugman, who has spent years arguing against "deficit scolds" for holding back economic and social progress, has emerged as a fierce critic of the MMT school. He's also expressed frustration with how the rules of MMT seem to keep changing, so criticizing it feels like shooting at an ever-moving target.[5]

For our purposes, it's worth considering the effect of MMT, which is to provide an intellectual framework for Democrats to sidestep questions about the debt implications of their proposals. One of the school's leading proponents, former Sanders' economic advisor Stephanie Kelton, counsels Democratic politicians that they shouldn't let questions about how to pay for proposals get in the way of making the case for a given policy on its merits.[6]

Some Democrats, including media sensation Rep. Alexandria Ocasio-Cortez, have explicitly cited MMT in response to questions about how to pay for their proposals.[7] Many others, without specifically citing MMT by name, have nonetheless internalized its teachings about downplaying the importance of debt concerns. For instance, Democratic presidential candidate Sen. Kamala Harris, when pressed on the staggering cost of some of her proposals said, "It's not about a cost. It's about an investment. And then the question should be, is it worth the cost in terms of the investment potential?"[8]

This shift is not surprising. Democratic proposals poll well until people are told about the tradeoffs. A good example is "Medicare for all," the latest branding for what is essentially a plan to socialize health insurance in America.[9] A January 2019 poll from the Kaiser Family Foundation found that 56 percent of Americans support the idea, compared with just 42 percent who oppose it. When told that it would "require most Americans to pay more in taxes," support drops to 37 percent while opposition shoots up to 60 percent.[10] So Democrats want as much as possible to emphasize the broad idea of free health care, while desperately avoiding questions about the costs. Dismissing concerns about costs makes it significantly easier for Democrats to frame any policy discussion around the parts of their proposals that are most popular.

The problems facing millennials that we've explored in this book can be divided into two broad categories: the crushing burden of the federal debt, and the rising living costs that have eaten up income gains, making it difficult to build wealth. Millennials could react in different ways. They could look at the staggering growth in the federal debt and become more worried about the size of government. Or, they could look to government to remedy their problems. They are increasingly choosing the latter path.

Polls have shown that generally speaking, millennials either do not care about the issue of the federal debt, or they deprioritize it relative to other issues. As a generation, they tend to be more liberal in general[11] and more welcoming of a larger role for the federal government. A Pew survey found that 57 percent of millennials said they prefer "a bigger government providing more services"; 67 percent agreed that it was "the federal government's responsibility to make sure all Americans have health coverage"; and 63 percent approved of Obamacare.[12] In all cases, that was well ahead of any other generation.

Though conservatives may decry the new wave of spending proposals from leading Democrats as "socialism," that label carries less stigma for millennials. In 2018, the GenForward Survey of the University of Chicago found that 45 percent of those aged 18 to 34 had a positive view of socialism, nearly as many as the 49 percent who had a positive view of capitalism. The same survey found 62 percent who said "we need a strong government to handle today's complex economic problems."[13] Another poll, conducted by YouGov on behalf of the Victims of Communism Memorial Foundation, was even more stark, finding that 52 percent of millennials said they would prefer to live in a socialist (46 percent) or actually communist (6 percent) country over a capitalist one, which was preferred by just 40 percent.[14] There may be no better demonstration of the change in perception of socialism than the success of Sanders himself among young voters, as he proudly embraces the modified label, "democratic socialism."

Millennials don't have the experience of having lived through the Cold War and many failed socialist experiments, but they did spend formidable years during the Great Recession, which they perceive as a consequence of the failures of capitalism. They are also facing daily struggles in their economic lives. Although many conservatives mock their concerns as overly whiny, the resurgent Left has promised that those struggles can be alleviated—if not eliminated—by government intervention.

At the same time, millennials have not yet faced the tangible consequences of the rising debt. The stark choices outlined in this book—significant tax increases, drastic benefits cuts, runaway inflation—have not actually happened yet. As explained in Chapter 3, nobody can point to a magic level of debt that suddenly triggers a fiscal crisis—economists only believe that the odds of such a crisis increase the greater the debt is, and the longer the United States continues without a plan to contain it. For now, however, bond markets have been willing to continue purchasing U.S. debt at low interest rates. While the debt burden does not currently seem to have a tangible effect on their daily lives, millennials are actually struggling to juggle health care, student loan payments, housing costs, child care, and so on. So they are increasingly susceptible to the straightforward message of those promising to have government step in and relieve their burdens.

Vast new government programs may come with a promise of fixing millennials' problems, but this is an illusion. The proposals would add tens of trillions of dollars in new spending over the next decade alone, exacerbating an already unsustainable debt problem, without solving the underlying issues.

For instance, the Sanders "Medicare for all" proposal that has been endorsed by four other Democrats seeking the party's nomination in 2020 (Sens. Harris, Elizabeth Warren, Cory Booker, and Kirsten Gillibrand) has been projected to increase federal spending by $32 trillion over the next decade. And that estimate isn't some wild right-wing analysis; it was the conclusion of the liberal Urban Institute.[15] To put that staggering figure into perspective, it's nearly triple what the already unsustainable Medicare program is supposed to spend over the next decade.[16] Measured another way, if the federal government were to collect double the individual and corporate income taxes each year between 2020 and 2029, lawmakers would still need to come up with an additional $5 trillion to finance the new spending.

That's just one proposal. The Brookings Institution–affiliated Hamilton Project estimated a job guarantee program with a $15 per hour minimum wage would cost about $409–$543 billion a year. That means the 10-year cost could exceed $5 trillion.[17] Warren wants to spend $1.2 trillion on her plan for free college and student loan forgiveness[18] and another $700 billion on child care (and that estimate is low, because it's only after accounting for promised economic benefits of the proposal).[19] Several candidates have embraced the sweeping Green New Deal to address the issue of climate change, which integrates many of the above proposals along with dramatic plans to move the United States to 100 percent renewable energy (from the current 17 percent)[20] within a decade.[21] Though no official cost estimate has been released for the blueprint, the American Action Forum, a right-of-center think tank run by former CBO director Doug Holtz-Eakin, took a stab at estimating the costs and came up with $51 trillion to $93 trillion. The wide range is a testament to different assumptions given the current lack of specifics in the proposal.[22] And remember, all of this spending is coming on top of the nearly $100 trillion in projected debt that's expected in the coming decades.

Democrats often try to argue that their proposals can be paid for simply by increasing taxes on the rich. Warren, for instance, has proposed a "wealth tax" on ultra-millionaires that would tax wealth above $50 million at an additional 2 percent, and above $1 billion at 3 percent.[23] She points to a study[24] done for her campaign that says the tax would raise $2.75 trillion. But the study does not take into account the likely economic distortion that would occur as wealthier individuals take measures to avert the tax. Lawrence Summers, the Clinton Treasury Secretary and Obama economic advisor, has made the case that a wealth tax is likely to raise a fraction of the $2.75 trillion, citing, among other things, evidence from estate taxes.[25] European socialist countries have tried wealth taxes but abandoned them because in practice they raised much less revenue than promised and were difficult to administer.[26] In France, socialists passed a wealth tax in the 1980s, but it led to an exodus of high net worth individuals over the decades, sucking revenue out of the country. One study estimated that 42,000 millionaires left the country between 2000 and 2014.[27] With the election of President Emmanuel Macron, France joined other countries in ditching it.[28]

Even if the wealth tax could raise the promised $2.75 trillion, however, that wouldn't even be enough to pay for an average year of "Medicare for all"—let alone the entire agenda being proposed by the resurgent Left. The liberal Economic Policy Institute has conceded that, "a spending commitment as large as single-payer health care requires more broad-based tax changes on top of" those targeting the top 3 percent of earners."[29]

Even putting aside the fiscal component for the moment, the proposals are no easy fixes to the underlying problems facing millennials.

For instance, the socialized health insurance proposal from Sanders would require kicking nearly 180 million people[30] off of their private health insurance within four years to put them on a new government-run plan.[31] That represents all those receiving coverage through their employers or purchasing coverage on their own. The proposal promises not only to cover everybody, and with more generous benefits, but also to have no premiums, copayments, or deductibles. This drastic expansion of demand for health care services is not met by a plan to increase the supply of doctors, hospitals, and other medical providers. In fact, the whole argument for such a plan is that it would save money by using the government's bargaining power to reduce payment rates. Doing this, however, would make the medical profession less profitable, if not completely unprofitable in some cases, such as in small rural hospitals. The end result of this would be that everybody would be issued a card that promises unlimited free health care, and yet in reality people would find it increasingly difficult to actually access care in a timely manner. Should government respond by increasing payment rates, it would only make the program that much more costly.

In contrast, millennials could benefit from free market health care reforms. Right now, as a legacy from World War II, most Americans with private coverage obtain their insurance through their employers, because of the special tax advantage. This makes much less sense in a world in which people often move from job-to-job or are self-employed. Also, under Obamacare, every American is forced to choose between expensive plans with mandated benefits they may not need, or go without any insurance at all. Under a reformed system, individuals could enjoy the same tax advantages for purchasing insurance on their own as they would by doing so through their employers, allowing them to take their insurance with them wherever they work. Also, they would be allowed to choose among a wide array of plans, at different price levels, depending on their medical needs. (For a more in-depth discussion of free market health care alternatives, see my previous book: *Overcoming Obamacare: Three Approaches to Reversing the Government Takeover of Healthcare.*)

On the issue of housing, instead of spending wildly on new affordable housing initiatives, policymakers could start by streamlining regulations, permitting, and land-use restrictions that create artificial barriers to the development of cheaper housing options. Even Democratic presidential candidate Sen. Cory Booker, as part of a housing plan that otherwise calls for vast new government spending to cap rent at 30 percent of income, acknowledges, "Across the country, cities and towns implement land-use restrictions that make it harder and more expensive to build new affordable housing. The result is fewer units and higher costs for renters."[32]

Policymakers could also look at ways to decrease the amount of licensing, certifications, and degree requirements that are imposed for many lines of work, creating barriers for people without the proper credentials from getting decent-paying jobs.

Solving the student debt problem by simply throwing more money at higher education is not an easy fix either.

As we saw in Chapter 2, the decision of the federal government to subsidize student loans was a significant driver of increased college costs in the first place.

Yet Democratic candidates have been in a bidding war to see how much more money they can pump into colleges and universities. In April, Warren proposed a plan to cancel up to $50,000 in student debt for everybody with household income under $100,000, then phase out the relief until households reach $250,000 of income, at which point they would no longer qualify for debt cancelation. Her campaign said this would cost $640 billion.[33] Not to be outdone, in June, Sanders proposed the total elimination of all student debt at the cost of $1.6 trillion.[34]

Cancelling student debt, as they propose, would create a moral hazard by signaling that people who make sacrifices to pay off their debt are suckers, because if they wait long enough, the government will just step in. Far from getting rid of the debt problem, it would just encourage current students to borrow even more money in hopes that theirs will eventually get cancelled too. And the flood of money would give a green light to schools to hike up their tuition even more.

Furthermore, as Reason's Peter Suderman among others, has noted, student loan forgiveness "is a massive giveaway to relatively well-off people." That is, those who have college degrees are relatively wealthier and more connected than those who do not, and this is who would be targeted with government largesse.[35] This is true under the Warren proposal, but even more true under the Sanders plan, which would wipe away the debt of graduate school as well, and have no income limits, so that working doctors and lawyers with six-figure salaries would have taxpayers footing the bill for their expensive educations.

It's easy to simply say that health care, and all other human needs, will be available for free and financed by a small number of millionaires. But in reality, the resurgent socialist vision for America would require massive tax increases on the middle class and it would be impossible to raise taxes enough to pay for these new initiatives without devastating economic consequences. Even if all this new spending were magically "paid for" by increasing taxes without any negative economic effects, the new spending would have eaten up revenue sources that would no longer be available to address the existing debt crisis.

The primary focus of this book has been laying out the tremendous burdens being placed on younger Americans and the extent to which baby boomers have used their power to block any real changes that might spare millennials from a grim economic future. This always triggers the inevitable follow up: What can be done to solve the problem?

The truth is that solutions, while involving a lot of complex and emotionally difficult issues, are at least conceptually fairly straightforward. Any plan to put the debt on a sustainable fiscal course involves reducing spending, increasing taxes, or instituting some combination of both approaches. There is no shortage of policy ideas that fall somewhere along this spectrum.

Paul Ryan wanted to demonstrate that the debt could become sustainable even while keeping tax rates at historical levels. His proposals relied on transitioning Medicare into a system in which seniors would receive a subsidy that would vary based on age and income, and allow them to choose among competing private plans. Former President Bush proposed allowing individuals to invest a portion of their Social Security payroll taxes in a market account.

Other proposals typically involve various adjustments to benefits or increases to the payroll taxes that fund the programs. For instance, the government could increase the retirement age, reflecting the fact that life expectancy has increased dramatically since Medicare and Social Security were created. Social Security's retirement age is in the process of gradually increasing to age 67 by 2027, but one could go beyond that without betraying the original purpose of the program. There are also ways to slow down the rate at which Social Security benefits grow, or to means test both programs so that wealthier Americans who aren't as dependent on Social Security or Medicare would receive fewer benefits.

In 2018, Brian Riedl of the Manhattan Institute set out a plan that aimed to stabilize the publicly held debt at 95 percent of GDP in the coming decades.[36] At first blush, that seems like a relatively modest goal. You may recall from

Chapter 3, that right now debt is at about 78 percent of GDP, which itself is the highest level since 1950, in the wake of World War II. What Riedl is proposing is to maintain peacetime debt at an even higher level, one that was only surpassed in the peak years of 1945 and 1946.

Riedl's plan integrates ideas including reducing benefits for those with higher incomes, a Ryan-style Medicare reform (though with more generous subsidies), and raising the Social Security retirement age. Though a former Republican staffer, Riedl has come around to the view that the fiscal math makes serious debt reduction too daunting without some amount of tax increases. So his plan contains about $1 of tax hikes for every $3 in reduced spending.

Those who want to shield Medicare and Social Security from changes as much as possible argue for much more significant tax increases. One idea being pushed by some liberals is to raise or eliminate the cap on payroll taxes, which hit the first $132,900 of salary in 2019.[37]

Though one could write extensively about the pros and cons of various reforms, the reality is that none of them are going anywhere until politics fundamentally change. And ultimately, millennials hold the key to making that happen. By the 2020 election, millennials will surpass baby boomers as the largest adult age generation, giving them significant political power.[38] If they were to actually take up the cause of tackling the federal debt, lawmakers would be forced to take it more seriously. At a minimum, their political power could provide an opposing force to the inertia that pushes lawmakers toward preserving the unsustainable status quo.

As we've seen, the United States is entering an era of unprecedented debt due to the costs of taking care of the baby boomers, who are standing in the way of reforms to the status quo. They will leave behind a mess to debt-saddled millennials, who are already struggling to build wealth and save for retirement. Absent action, millennials risk a catastrophic crisis that will force them to choose among sudden and drastic spending cuts, crushing tax increases, runaway inflation, national security vulnerability, economic disaster, or some combination of all of them. Millennials have the power to force lawmakers to make the necessary changes to avoid this outcome. But nothing will change unless they learn about the consequences of the looming crisis and resist the allure of politicians promising that government will solve all their problems.

They could, of course, choose to ignore the problem as their predecessors did. They could increase the obligations government is taking on and hope that investors continue to finance the federal debt at low interest rates in perpetuity. But if they were to take that gamble, even if they averted disaster in the near term, they'd just be kicking the can farther down the road, and imposing more burdens on the generations that come after them. Essentially, they'd be doing to younger generations what they complain baby boomers have done to them.

PART 2

 ≈

Dissenting Points of View

CHAPTER 6

Millennials: America's Luckiest Generation

❮❯

DAVID HARSANYI

EVERY GENERATION faces a unique set of challenges, but no generation has ever faced as few serious challenges as millennials. By nearly every quantifiable measure, Americans born between the early 1980s and mid-to-late 1990s have enjoyed the most peaceful, wealthiest, safest era in our history. And being the most educated and globally connected people the world has ever known, means you don't engender a lot of sympathy from the old folks.

Of course, making sweeping statements about any arbitrary generational grouping, while quite fun, can also be a ham-fisted proposition. Americans, after all, are diverse, with diverse experiences and diverse expectations. No one lives in a utopia. Everyone makes tradeoffs. Still, the constant grousing about the unprecedented hardships millennials face is in dire need of historical perspective. The deck, my young friends, is not stacked against you.

"Millennials," as Philip Klein points out, "face twin challenges—chasing rising living costs and absorbing unprecedented federal debt." More than 80 percent of mil-lennial workers say they're worried Social Security won't be there for them, according to a recent study by the Transa-merica Center for Retirement.[1]

It is inarguable that the debt crisis will have to be dealt with, and that the crisis is our fault. Millennials, and subse-quent generations, will be compelled to make tough policy choices regarding the massive self-perpetuating inter-gen-erational debt-ridden programs like Social Security and Medicare. They will do so because of the profligate and irre-sponsible choices of the boomers and Generation Xers like myself.

However, the lesson learned by millennials hasn't been that socialization of retirement funding was a big mistake. Rather, it seems, they have, in large numbers, been convinced that we need massive self-perpetuating inter-generational debt-ridden programs. This is why Klein was compelled to write this excellent book detailing the destructive long-term consequences of big-ticket programs that promise "free" things.

Klein posits that millennials face the prospects of "crush-ing tax increases, massive inflation, sky high interest rates, and sudden, significant cuts to retirement programs when they reach their twilight years." As the author himself lays out, however, there are options millennials have to mitigate this fate.

We are no longer talking about children, after all. The

oldest millennials are already approaching 40. These are Americans who have a political portfolio that illustrates no more concern about spending than previous generations—perhaps even less. A 2017 Millennial Impact Report found that the top political concerns of millennials are civil rights/racial discrimination, employment, health care reform, climate change, immigration, education, and well, there is nothing concerning government debt or spending anywhere on the list.[2] Millennials are already complicit. If history teaches us anything, it's that they will reject bold measures and embrace the rock-ribbed traditional American pastime of passing incremental and weak reforms and punting the crisis to future generations.

American life is a continuum. Our problems don't neatly fold into generational time slots. All of us have grappled with issues left us by previous generations. When we take a holistic view of American life, we learn that millennials have few legitimate reasons to be resentful. Their inheritance is the most impressive.

Consider: Baby boomers left millennials with growing debt, but also with the greatest technological revolution in information and commerce in history, one even more consequential than the printing revolution. Millennials tend to dismiss the affordable mobile supercomputer in their hands as nothing more than a cheap gadget. Perhaps those who spend their entire lives with instantaneous access to a world of commerce, music, art, literature, data, news, statistics, sports—all human knowledge, basically— don't realize just how much the world has changed.

There are tens of millions of Americans who remember cracking open encyclopedias for even the most rudimentary information and driving to a Radio Shack to buy floppy discs for their expensive, but largely useless, computers. For that matter, there are tens of millions of Americans who remember the prospects of joining a workforce propelled by repetitive menial labor jobs in factories and farms. They remember days when college was largely reserved for the wealthy. They remember gas lines and the depressive political and economic environment of the 1970s. Yet, inexplicably, many people still pine for these days because of the alleged stability it provided.

Are millennials poorer than other generations at the same point? In some ways, yes. The driving reason for this disparity is a penchant for delaying traditional adult milestones. As a group, millennials are prone to choose short-term happiness and independence over long-term wealth accumulation. These are choices made in part because of changing societal norms. This doesn't necessarily mean that millennials are more irresponsible than previous generations, but rather that they are willing to defer financial rewards. Not everything is about money.

Two ways millennials do this is by attending college and delaying marriage.

According to Pew Research Center, 68 percent of early

boomers and 62 percent of late boomers were married by the age of 37. For Generation X it was 57 percent. But it is only 46 percent for millennials.[3] This means millennials aren't taking advantage of economies of scale, pooled savings, shared work duties, resources, and intellectual ability. They delay the stability of family life.

Now, perhaps millennials are leading more satisfying lives than their parents and grandparents—these things are difficult to quantify. But comparing themselves economically with generations that embraced a different set of priorities and lived in a far less dynamic economy at the same age is misleading.

Are some things more expensive these days? Sure. Mostly because those things are better.

"In the past several decades, the cost of health care in the United States has undergone dramatic growth, easily outpacing the expansion of the economy during the same time period," writes Klein. The health care they get has also outpaced expectations in dramatic ways, as well. Expensive medical advances—ones that will almost certainly become cheaper as millennials age—have been worth the cost. We live longer, more productive lives with less pain and fewer threats because of modern medicine.

Take the death rate from cancer in the United States, which has precipitously declined over the past decades. Because of reductions in smoking and technologies that allow for early detection and treatment, the American Cancer Society says that the survival rate has increased by 25 percent from its peak in 1991.[4] Not only are diseases that once endangered average Americans, like smallpox and polio, now obsolete, newer ones, like AIDS/HIV, may soon be eliminated.[5]

And yes, college is more expensive, as well. It is also more accessible to far more people. Back in 1965, only 5.9 million Americans were enrolled in college—and it was mostly the wealthy. By the time the first millennials were born, over 13 million were enrolled in institutions of higher education. By 2010, there were 21 million Americans enrolled. According to the Federal Reserve study, millennials are the most educated generation, with 65 percent of them possessing at least an associate degree.[6]

One imagines boomers, most of whom had been compelled to go directly to work after high school, would eagerly have taken on loans to be able to study in the broad array fields that are now available to students. Unlike millennials, many of them would likely have chosen more useful degrees in affordable, less-prestigious, and less-expensive schools.

Buying a house can also be prohibitively expensive. Many millennials choose to live in urban areas and with high rents in highly sought after neighborhoods that are safer, cleaner, and more vibrant than they were 40, 30, or even 20 years ago.

For those millennials who do choose to buy a home—with historically low-interest rate mortgages!—it will be, in every measurable way, safer and more comfortable than the one their parents and grandparents grew up in. The average square footage of a poorly heated, non-air conditioned, light-deprived, and badly insulated home in 1950 was 983 square feet. In 1970 it was 1,500 square feet. In 1990, 2,080. And in 2014 it was 2,657 square feet. If you live in the suburbs, you live in a veritable castle.[7] And as Klein notes, the size of the families that live in those houses is smaller than ever.

The growth of the upper middle class—something we rarely hear about—has skewed the national average of home ownership.[8] Yes, the median home value in areas around Washington DC, New York City, and Los Angeles skew above half a million dollars. But the median price of a three-bedroom home in Des Moines, Iowa is $139,500.[9] In Fort Worth, $197,500.[10] In Charlotte, it's $225,500.[11] There are plenty of reasonable options in localities outside of the main metropolitan areas.

Does this mean that millennials shouldn't worry about the cost of a higher education, health care, and housing? Of course not. These are legitimate concerns. Young people often start out with debt, and that's a burden, as well. No generation views their everyday situation through the prism of history. Millennials shouldn't be expected to say, "Boy, I'm happy I didn't have to go to Vietnam" when paying their exorbitant rent.

However, the notion that this plaintive millennial generation has toiled in uniquely grueling economic conditions because they have to pay for top-of-the-line futuristic health care, virtual mansions, and a college experience that others could only dream about, exhibits an extraordinarily narrow understanding of history. Furthermore, unlike most generations that preceded it, millennials have the ability fix their problems without bloodshed or perilous society-disrupting events.

So how about a little appreciation?

CHAPTER 7
Fear Less

$>\!\!<$

RAMESH PONNURU

PHILIP KLEIN'S description of millennials' economic future is sufficiently grim. It is possible to be significantly more optimistic while still finding reasons for alarm.

He is all too persuasive about the uncontrolled trajectory of federal entitlement programs and (therefore) of the national debt. Both Republicans and Democrats have been moving in the wrong direction on entitlements, with the former less committed than ever to reform and the latter more eager than they have been in a generation to expand them. The longer we avoid bringing future costs and revenues into rational alignment, the more wrenching the needed change will be.

In three respects, however, millennials may have brighter prospects than Klein allows.

First, the Census Bureau, on which Klein relies for some of his most dire statistics regarding trends in income over the last several decades, has overestimated inflation over time and therefore underestimated progress. The bureau's numbers indicate that the median income for men fell by 14 percent from 1974 through 2018. A measure that better accounts for the way people can shift their consumption to blunt the effects of inflation on their welfare eliminates most of that decline.[1]

Immigrants taking low-wage jobs pulled down that median, even if they themselves were making gains (and even if they were not reducing anyone else's wages). Correcting for that phenomenon, and isolating the wages of native-born workers, would almost certainly show a modest increase in median wages among men and a dramatic one among women. As Klein notes, the numbers would look even better if they included non-wage benefits.[2]

Second, our worries about student debt should also be put in perspective. College graduates in their 30s and early 40s spend an average 1.4 percent of their income repaying student loans.[3] That percentage has been rising, but so have the wages of college graduates. Getting the diploma may lead to debt, but the diploma is a valuable asset on the other side of the ledger—albeit one that does not show up in the calculations of a generation's net worth.

Student debt is, to be sure, a major burden for some households. Young people who accrued debt without attaining college degrees have a particular problem, because the wages of that group tend to be closer to those of high-school rather than college graduates.[4] But to note this fact is already to suggest that the size of someone's student loan debt is a poor proxy for the extent to which our education system has served him or her badly.

Third, fears about millennials' retirement saving may well be overstated. Our available data are not as helpful in evaluating this question as we might wish. But a 2015 study suggested that the average age at which people start saving for retirement has continued to fall over the decades.[5] The 401(k) system has been improving, with lower fees and more widespread use of auto-enrollment. It's true that young people will almost certainly have to put in more years in the labor force than their grandparents. Yet even that necessity has its bright side; part of the additional work that will be required is because the young will be living longer and therefore will have to finance longer retirements than their grandparents did.

Another reason millennials will have to work longer is to make up for the shortfall in Social Security and Medicare. That brings us back to the great weakness in our retirement system: its government-run components, including both the old-age entitlements and pensions for public-sector workers. In the private sector, running pensions using the actuarial standards that prevail in the public sector would lead to prison sentences. Instead our collective malfeasance will entail its own collective punishment, with the precise form depending on choices we have yet to make.

The most feasible solutions that Left, Right, and Center have offered for the insolvency of entitlements all require sacrifice from millennials (and their successors, currently labeled Generation Z). Perhaps high-income millennials will have to pay higher taxes, as the Left wants; perhaps they will have to accept lower benefit levels, as the Right does; and perhaps they will have pay in both ways. Working lives will likely, as mentioned, be extended.

Millennials could still end up with higher lifetime incomes, on average, than their parents; whether or not they do will depend largely on how quickly productivity rises in the future. But their incomes will be lower than if they did not have to finance the unfunded retirement costs of previous generations. If we accept that prudence requires us to close the gap over the next several decades, a blow to the millennials is unavoidable. (If we continue to opt for imprudence, as Klein points out, millennials may pay in more drastic ways.)

We can, however, dig the pit deeper. Nearly all Democrats in the House of Representatives have endorsed a bill to expand Social Security benefits. To their credit, their legislation aims to close the program's financing gap. But even if one assumes (dubiously) that the higher tax rates will succeed in the goal of creating fiscal balance, the bill would make the generational imbalance worse. The expanded benefits would begin quickly, so that baby boomers who are already getting more money from the program than they contributed to it would reap an even bigger windfall. Millennials will have to pay higher taxes to finance their own expanded benefits, plus even higher taxes to finance more generosity to their elders.

It would be easy for millennials who are familiar with this information to blame the baby boomers for stealing their futures, and some have yielded to the temptation. It is not wholly unfair to blame them for millennials' problems. The boomers have had immense influence for a long time, and few of them used it to try to make entitlements work better for future generations.

On the other hand, the problem was largely one they themselves had inherited. The key decision that has unbalanced Social Security was made in the late 1970s, when initial benefits were set to rise automatically rather than only when Congress legislated increases. Most of the major decisionmakers at the time were not baby boomers. In the 1980s, a bipartisan deal extended the program's solvency by raising taxes and slowly raising the retirement age. The boomers took the brunt of both changes and have ended up with a worse ratio of benefits to taxes than their predecessors had.

Our inheritances from previous generations are almost always mixed and complex, just as generations themselves are. The boomers were born into an America that now seems in some ways to have been an idyll, with rapid economic growth and familial stability. But they were also the first generation to grow up with the fear of nuclear war. They entered the workforce at a time when postwar America seemed to be breaking down amid stagflation, a crime wave, riots and assassinations, a disastrous war, and four prematurely ended presidencies in a row.

They could have blamed their own parents for the problems that beset them, and many of them did. To the considerable extent that boomers overcame those problems, though, it was not because they were spurred by anger or resentment toward their elders.

We should take care not to nourish these sentiments, which are both unjustified and unproductive, by exaggerating the millennial plight. The boomers themselves are, oddly enough, partly responsible for this gloom. Our politics at the moment is suffused by a kind of bitter nostalgia, a sense of lost possibility, that owes a lot to the cultural dominance of the boomers and their tendency not to accept the realities of aging. Thus, we interpret millennial prospects against the backdrop of a heightened fear of national decline.

The millennials face some real economic challenges. Those of us who are older than they are should do what we can to help them through those challenges. All of us should start with gratitude for the country we have, and realism about the imperfections every generation is dealt. It is important that we redesign our entitlements and adapt our economy. But it is more important still that we honor our fathers and mothers.

CHAPTER 8

A Response to David Harsanyi and Ramesh Ponnuru

———————— ≥≤ ————————

I WANT TO THANK David Harsanyi and Ramesh Ponnuru for taking the time to offer such thoughtful responses to my work. Both contributors present alternate ways of looking at the state of millennials. Although each of them agrees with me that the trajectory of federal debt is worrisome and unsustainable, both argue, from different angles, that I overstate the case about millennial struggles when it comes to their personal finances while overlooking other advantages enjoyed by the generation. Harsanyi is especially less sympathetic to their complaints. I hope that by considering the data I marshalled, and then digesting the responses, readers will come away with a more complete picture on this important topic.

Having read their responses, there are a few things I'd want to add. Ponnuru graciously argues that we should be a bit easier on the baby boomers. I find it much harder to be so forgiving. Even if one grants that many decisions that put us on the current fiscal course were made before baby boomers came to power, it's difficult to forgive them for failing to address a predictable crisis that has been staring everybody in the face. They were not innocent bystanders. Baby boomers have been the dominant political force in the United States for decades. If we include Barack Obama (who was born in 1961, technically late in the era), baby boomers have held the presidency for the past quarter century and counting. They had the power to reform unsustainable programs or perpetuate and expand them, and they chose the later course.

Harsanyi has much less patience for the grievances of the millennials than either Ponnuru or me. I will largely let my analysis of their financial headwinds in Chapter 2 speak for itself. But I would note that it is troublesome for those who believe in a limited role for the federal government to be so dismissive of the concerns of this generation. Harsanyi laments that, "the lesson learned by millennials hasn't been that socialization of retirement funding was a big mistake. Rather, it seems, they have, in large numbers, been convinced that we need massive self-perpetuating inter-generational debt-ridden programs."

As I write in this book, especially in the final chapter, this is certainly where things are trending. But I also don't think it should be treated as a *fait accompli*. If there is any hope at all of trying to contain the growth of government and avoid the slide toward socialism, this generation is going to have to be convinced there's a better path. The reality is that millennials are going to be the dominant voting bloc in America for a long time. And if those who believe in limiting government won't even acknowledge some of the challenges they're facing and offer solutions, it's inevitable which way they'll go. If one side is telling millennials to essentially stop whining, and the other side is speaking sympathetically about their problems and promising to alleviate them, it's pretty clear which side they are going to choose.

The center-Right often makes the same mistake of failing to acknowledge problems and to offer tangible solutions until it's too late, allowing those on the Left to fill the vacuum with ideas that involve expanding government. Those on the Right are often forced to play catch-up on policy because they wait until Democratic presidents are proposing something to jump on issues. This can be seen especially when it comes to health care policy, one of the issues Harsanyi highlights.

Harsanyi acknowledges that health care spending has grown over time, but argues that we should also consider how quality has improved. Although this is true, what's left unexplored is the fact that in other areas of the economy (such as the examples of mobile phones and computer technology that Harsanyi cites), improvements in quality have been accompanied by reductions in price. Today's computers and televisions are not just significantly better than the ones of yesteryear, but they are also much cheaper. But this has not been the case in health care, an area in which improvements in quality have been accompanied by dramatic cost increases. The difference is that there is no free market for health care, in which consumers can harness their purchasing power to demand better prices. This is the result of a web of destructive policies that, over time, deprived consumers of the incentives to seek cheaper care, while muffling price signals.

I explored this in more detail in my previous book, *Overcoming Obamacare*, but it's important to note here that there were several openings for those on the Right to make the case for a consumer-driven, market-based approach to health care. Instead, what happened is that they mainly ignored the issue by either downplaying the problems in the system or releasing half-baked alternatives—and even those were typically presented only after waiting for liberals to attempt to address health care. After they successfully defeated President Clinton's health care push in 1994, Republicans largely went into hibernation on the issue—only to awake in 2009 to launch a failed effort to stop Obamacare. After the passage of Obamacare, during their time out of power, Republicans spent four election cycles running on promises to "repeal and replace" Obamacare without coalescing around their own alternative. Predictably, in 2017, when Republicans finally had unified control of Washington, they could not settle on legislation and their repeal and replace effort went down in flames. As we enter the 2020 election, Obamacare is fully entrenched, and as liberals move on to embrace full on socialized health insurance, Republicans are further than ever from articulating a competing vision.

This is what I fear will happen more broadly if we simply write off a whole generation as a lost cause and fail to appreciate their legitimate concerns. It would be much better to try and grapple with their challenges and steer them in a more prudent direction.

Acknowledgments

⋝⋜

I HAVE BEEN INTERESTED in writing a book on the monumental burden facing younger Americans for over a decade, so I was intrigued when Keith Urbahn at Javelin mentioned that Templeton Press was interested in publishing something on the subject. Through subsequent conversations with Susan Arellano it became clear that we shared the same vision for a book that would deal sympathetically with the plight of millennials.

I am grateful to Keith for bringing me the project and Susan's efforts to steer me toward writing a book that was adequately detailed to be of interest to the policy community while being concise and straightforward enough to speak to a broader audience. I would like to thank Trish Vergilio for shepherding the book along the production process and Dan Reilly for his insights on the best ways to market the book to its target audience.

This book would not be possible were it not for the *Washington Examiner*, where I have always had the freedom to write about policy issues in a serious way under the leadership of Hugo Gurdon. Being able to write about politics and policy on a daily basis provided the foundation for me to write this book.

I would also like to thank David Harsanyi and Ramesh Ponnuru for agreeing to contribute to the project with such thoughtful responses.

Finally, and above all, I would like to thank my wife for her help and support throughout the writing process.

Notes

— ≳≲ —

Notes to the Introduction

1. Harvard Kennedy School Institute of Politics, "Survey of Young Americans' Attitudes toward Politics and Public Service 35th Edition," March 8-25, 2018, Question 20A, https://iop.harvard.edu/sites/default/files/content/Release%202%20Toplines.pdf.

2. The term "millennial," like descriptions of other age cohorts such as the "Silent Generation" or "Generation X," is one that was adopted by sociologists and that doesn't have a clear start date and end date. In 2015, a U.S. Census Bureau report on millennials overtaking baby boomers in terms of population size, informally described millennials as "America's youth born between 1982 and 2000", although the bureau does not officially define any generation aside from the baby boomers. The Pew Research Center, in contrast, defines the group as being born between 1981 and 1996. For the purposes of this book, when referring to a specific study or piece of data, I denoted the specific ages or years studied. Otherwise, when referring to millennials in a more general way, I mean the group born roughly between the early 1980s and mid-to-late 1990s. [See: "Millennials Outnumber Baby Boomers and Are Far More Diverse, Census Bureau Reports," June 25, 2015. https://www.census.gov/newsroom/press-releases/2015/cb15-113.html; Michael Dimock, "Defining generations: Where Millennials end and Generation Z begins," Pew Research Center, Jan. 17, 2019. https://www.pewresearch.org/fact-tank/2019/01/17/where-millennials-end-and-generation-z-begins/.]

3. Hamlet, Act III, Scene 1.

4. David Grossman, "How Do NASA's Apollo Computers Stack Up to an iPhone?," *Popular Mechanics,* March 13, 2017. https://www

.popularmechanics.com/space/moon-mars/a25655/nasa-computer
-iphone-comparison/.

5. Baby boomers are those born between 1946 and 1964, a period
   marked by sustained high birth rates in the U.S. [See: Sandra L. Colby
   and Jennifer M. Ortman, "The Baby Boom Cohort in the United
   States," (United States Census Bureau, Current Population Reports,
   May 2014), Figures 1, 3. https://www.census.gov/prod/2014pubs/p25-
   1141.pdf.]

6. Richard Fry, "Millennials projected to overtake Baby Boomers as
   America's largest generation," Pew Research Center, March 1, 2018. http
   ://www.pewresearch.org/fact-tank/2018/04/03/millennials-approach
   -baby-boomers-as-largest-generation-in-u-s-electorate/.

CHAPTER 1

1. Congressional Budget Office, "The 2019 Long-Term Budget Outlook,"
   June 2019. https://www.cbo.gov/system/files/2019-06/55331-LTBO-2
   .pdf.

2. CBO, "Long-Term Budget Projections," Jan. 2019, https://www.cbo
   .gov/about/products/budget-economic-data#1.

3. CBO, "The 2018 Long-Term Budget Outlook," June 2018, 1. https://
   www.cbo.gov/system/files/2018-06/53919-2018ltbo.pdf.

4. *Ibid.*, 2-3. https://www.cbo.gov/system/files/2018-06/53919-2018ltbo
   .pdf.

5. Social Security Administration, "Number of beneficiaries receiving benefits on Dec. 31, 1970-2018." https://www.ssa.gov/oact/STATS/OASDI
   benies.html.

6. Juliette Cubanski and Tricia Neuman, "The Facts on Medicare Spending and Financing," *Kaiser Family Foundation*, Jun 22, 2018. https://
   www.kff.org/report-section/the-facts-on-medicare-spending
   -and-financing-issue-brief-7305-12/.

CHAPTER 2

1. Richard Fry, "Young adult households are earning more than most
   older Americans did at the same age," Pew Research Center, Dec.

11, 2018. http://www.pewresearch.org/fact-tank/2018/12/11/young-adult-households-are-earning-more-than-most-older-americans-did-at-the-same-age/.

2. Christopher Kurz, Geng Li, and Daniel J. Vine, *Are Millennials Different?*, Finance and Economics Discussion Series 2018-080, Washington: Board of Governors of the Federal Reserve System, 3. https://www.federalreserve.gov/econres/feds/files/2018080pap.pdf.

3. Pew Research Center, "The rise in dual-income families," June 15, 2016. https://www.pewresearch.org/fact-tank/2018/06/13/fathers-day-facts/ft_16-06-14_fathersday_dual_income/.

4. Search of "The Care Index," an interactive map allowing users to look at the cost of child care across the U.S. https://www.care.com/care-index.

5. "This is how much child care costs in 2018," Care.com, https://www.care.com/c/stories/2423/how-much-does-child-care-cost/.

6. Kaiser Family Foundation, "Health Insurance Marketplace Calculator." https://www.kff.org/interactive/subsidy-calculator/.

7. Mark J. Perry, "New US homes today are 1,000 square feet larger than in 1973 and living space per person has nearly doubled," *American Enterprise Institute* (June 5, 2016). http://www.aei.org/publication/new-us-homes-today-are-1000-square-feet-larger-than-in-1973-and-living-space-per-person-has-nearly-doubled/.

8. Candace Taylor, "A Growing Problem in Real Estate: Too Many Too Big Houses," *Wall Street Journal*, March 21, 2019. https://www.wsj.com/articles/a-growing-problem-in-real-estate-too-many-too-big-houses-11553181782.

9. Annie Nova, "Waiting longer to buy a house could hurt millennials in retirement," CNBC, Oct. 25, 2018. https://www.cnbc.com/2018/10/25/the-homeownership-rate-is-falling-among-millennials-heres-why.html.

10. Alice H. Munnell and Wenliang Hou, "Will Millennials Be Ready for Retirement?", *Center for Retirement Research*, January 2018. https://crr.bc.edu/briefs/will-millennials-be-ready-for-retirement/.

11. U.S. Department of Housing and Urban Development, "Regulatory Barriers and Affordable Housing,", *Evidence Matters*, Spring 2018, 4–5.

12. Lyman Stone, "The Boomers Ruined Everything," *The Atlantic*, June 24, 2019. https://www.theatlantic.com/ideas/archive/2019/06/boomers-are-blame-aging-america/592336/.

13. Lyman Stone, "Red, White, and Gray: Population Aging, Deaths of Despair, and the Institutional Stagnation of America," *American Enterprise Institute*, June 2019, 14.

14. Lyman Stone, "The Boomers Ruined Everything," *The Atlantic*, June 24, 2019. https://www.theatlantic.com/ideas/archive/2019/06/boomers-are-blame-aging-america/592336/.

15. In the interest of keeping everything constant to 2018 dollars, this example uses the current federal minimum wage of $7.25 per hour. Many states have minimum wages higher than this amount.

16. Richard Fry, "The Growth in Student Debt," Pew Research Center, Oct. 7, 2014. http://www.pewsocialtrends.org/2014/10/07/the-growth-in-student-debt/.

17. Laura Feiveson, Alvaro Mezza, and Kamila Sommer, "Student Loan Debt and Aggregate Consumption Growth," FEDS Notes, Washington: Board of Governors of the Federal Reserve System, Feb. 21, 2018. https://www.federalreserve.gov/econres/notes/feds-notes/student-loan-debt-and-aggregate-consumption-growth-20180221.htm.

18. Board of Governors of the Federal Reserve System (US), Motor Vehicle Loans Owned and Securitized, Outstanding [MVLOAS], retrieved from FRED, Federal Reserve Bank of St. Louis. https://fred.stlouisfed.org/series/MVLOAS, April 27, 2019, Board of Governors of the Federal Reserve System (US), Student Loans Owned and Securitized, Outstanding [SLOAS], retrieved from FRED, Federal Reserve Bank of St. Louis; https://fred.stlouisfed.org/series/SLOAS, April 27, 2019; Board of Governors of the Federal Reserve System, Consumer Credit – G. 19 release, April 5, 2019. https://www.federalreserve.gov/releases/g19/Current/; Federal Reserve Bank of New York, Household Debt and Credit Report (Q4 2018) https://www.newyorkfed.org/microeconomics/hhdc.html.

19. *Credit card outstanding in the U.S.*, The Nilson Report, Jan. 2019.

20. Anthony Cilluffo, "5 facts about student loans," Pew Research Center, Aug. 24, 2017. https://www.pewresearch.org/fact-tank/2017/08/24/5-facts-about-student-loans/.

21. Alice H. Munnell and Wenliang Hou, "Will Millennials Be Ready for Retirement?", Center for Retirement Research, January 2018. https://crr.bc.edu/briefs/will-millennials-be-ready-for-retirement/.

22. Preston Cooper, "How Unlimited Student Loans Drive Up Tuition," *Forbes*, Feb. 22, 2017. https://www.forbes.com/sites/prestoncooper2/2017/02/22/how-unlimited-student-loans-drive-up-tuition/#5d8d301d52b6.

23. Greg Gordon and Aaron Hedlund, *Accounting for the Rise in College Tuition*, Working Paper 21967, National Bureau of Economic Research, Feb. 2016, 40. https://www.nber.org/papers/w21967.pdf.

24. College Board, "Trends in Student Aid 2018," Figures 15 and 16. https://trends.collegeboard.org/student-aid/figures-tables/loans.

25. Jaison R. Abel and Richard Deitz, "Do the Benefits of College Still Outweigh the Costs?" *Current Issues in Economics and Finance*, Federal Reserve Bank of New York, Vol. 20, No. 3, 4. https://www.newyorkfed.org/medialibrary/media/research/current_issues/ci20-3.pdf.

26. Sam Levin, "Millionaire tells millennials: if you want a house, stop buying avocado toast," *The Guardian*, May 15, 2017. https://www.theguardian.com/lifeandstyle/2017/may/15/australian-millionaire-millennials-avocado-toast-house.

27. William Cummings, "Millionaire to Millennials: Your avocado toast addiction is costing you a house," *USA Today*, May 16, 2017. https://www.usatoday.com/story/money/2017/05/16/millionaire-tells-millennials-your-avocado-addiction-costing-you-house/101727712/.

28. Bloomberg, "Why Millennials Are Ditching Credit Cards," Feb. 27, 2018. http://fortune.com/2018/02/27/why-millennials-are-ditching-credit-cards/.

29. Nathaniel Popper, "How Millennials Became Spooked by Credit Cards," *New York Times*, Aug. 14, 2016. https://www.nytimes.com/2016/08/15/business/dealbook/why-millennials-are-in-no-hurry-to-take-on-debt.html.

30. Credit Card Accountability Responsibility and Disclosure Act of 2009, Public Law 111–24, May 22, 2009. https://www.ftc.gov/sites/default/files/documents/statutes/credit-card-accountability-responsibility-and-disclosure-act-2009-credit-card-act/credit-card-pub-l-111-24_0.pdf.

31. Scott Graham, "Banks Spend $83 Million to Promote Student Credit

Card Use," *Huffington Post*, Nov. 4, 2010. https://www.huffpost.com/entry/banks-spend-83-million-to_b_778709.

32. Board of Governors of the Federal Reserve System, "Survey of Consumer Finances," 2016, Table 13. https://www.federalreserve.gov/econres/scfindex.htm.

33. Ibid.

34. Author interview.

35. Ibid.

36. Alan Kline, "Why point-of-sale lending is hot right now," *American Banker*, Feb. 7, 2018. https://www.americanbanker.com/news/why-point-of-sale-lending-is-hot-right-now.

37. Transunion, "Digitalization Among Factors Pushing Millennial Credit Preferences Toward Auto and Personal Loans," Aug. 30, 2017. https://newsroom.transunion.com/image/millennialgraphicfinal.jpg?10000.

38. "Generation Revealed: Decoding Millennial financial health," TransUnion, 2017, 7.

39. Kevin Morrison, "Loyalty and Rewards in the Digital Age: U.S. Consumer Credit Card Rewards Survey," *Aite*, Feb. 1, 2018. https://www.aitegroup.com/report/loyalty-and-rewards-digital-age-us-consumer-credit-card-rewards-survey.

40. Reuters, "US lottery operators worry as fewer millennials line up to play," Feb. 10, 2017. https://www.cnbc.com/2017/02/10/us-lottery-operators-worry-as-fewer-millennials-line-up-to-play.html.

41. Elizabeth Renter, "Millennials: How Much Are You Really Spending?" *Nerd Wallet*, Sept. 22, 2017. https://www.nerdwallet.com/blog/finance/millennials-how-much-are-you-really-spending/.

42. Northwestern Mutual, "Planning and Progress Study 2018." https://news.northwesternmutual.com/planning-and-progress-2018.

43. NBC News/GenForward, March 2018 Toplines, 9. https://genforward-survey.com/assets/uploads/2018/04/NBC-GenForward-March-2018-Toplines.pdf.

44. Navient, *Money Under 35*, 2017, 39, 41, 43. https://about.navient.com/Images/Money-Under-35-report-2017_tcm7-2871.pdf.

45. Ibid, 41.

46. Ibid., 43.

47. Alice H. Munnell and Wenliang Hou, "Will Millennials Be Ready for Retirement?", Center for Retirement Research, January 2018, 7.

48. Febaba R. Addo, Jason N. Houle, and Sharon Sassler, "The Changing Nature of the Association Between Student Loan Debt and Marital Behavior in Young Adulthood," *Journal of Family and Economic Issues*, Vol. 40, Issue 1, 86-101. https://link.springer.com/article/10.1007/s10834-018-9591-6.

49. Alice H. Munnell and Wenliang Hou, "Will Millennials Be Ready for Retirement?", Center for Retirement Research, January 2018. https://crr.bc.edu/briefs/will-millennials-be-ready-for-retirement/.

50. Matthew S. Rutledge, Geoffrey T. Sanzenbacher, and Francis M. Vitagliano, "How Does Student Debt Affect Early-Career Retirement Saving?" Center for Retirement Research, 2. http://crr.bc.edu/wp-content/uploads/2016/09/wp_2016-9_rev.pdf.

51. Ibid.

52. Matthew S. Rutledge, Geoffrey T. Sanzenbacher, and Francis M. Vitagliano, *How Does Student Debt Affect Early-Career Retirement Saving?* Center for Retirement Research, http://crr.bc.edu/wp-content/uploads/2016/09/wp_2016-9_rev.pdf.

53. Alice H. Munnell, Wenliang Hou, and Anthony Webb, *Will the Explosion of Student Debt Widen the Retirement Security Gap?*, http://crr.bc.edu/wp-content/uploads/2016/01/IB_16-2.pdf.

54. The one notable exception was 20- to 22-year-olds. This makes sense, as late baby boomers who were 20 to 22 in 1983 would have been entering the workforce in the middle of a major recession in 1981 and 1982, that saw unemployment peak at 10.8 percent, and remain in double digits until the summer of 1983. [See historical unemployment data from the Bureau of Labor Statistics. https://data.bls.gov/timeseries/LNS14000000.]

55. Board of Governors of the Federal Reserve System, "Survey of Consumer Finances", Table 4 https://www.federalreserve.gov/econres/scfindex.htm.

Chapter 3

1. George W. Bush, State of the Union Address, Feb. 5, 2005 https://www.americanrhetoric.com/speeches/stateoftheunion2005.htm.

2. The 2019 Annual Report of the Board of Trustees of the Federal Old-Age and Survivors Insurance and Federal Disability Insurance Trust

Funds, April 22, 2019, 3, 5. https://www.ssa.gov/OACT/TR/2019/tr2019.pdf.

3. Ibid., 5.

4. 2019 Annual Report of the Boards of Trustees of the Federal Hospital Insurance and Federal Supplementary Medical Insurance Trust Funds, April 22, 2019, 4, 27, 198.

5. 2019 Annual Report of the Boards of Trustees of the Federal Hospital Insurance and Federal Supplementary Medical Insurance Trust Funds, April 22, 2019, 4.

6. Ibid., 27.

7. CBO long-term budget projections, "Annual Data for Key Projections."

8. CBO, *The 2019 Long-Term Budget Outlook*, June 2019, 38-42. https://www.cbo.gov/system/files/2019-06/55331-LTBO-2.pdf.

9. Ibid., 45–47.

10. CBO, *The Budget and Economic Outlook: 2019 to 2029*, January 2019, Table 1-1, 7. https://www.cbo.gov/system/files?file=2019-01/54918-Outlook.pdf.

11. CBO, *The 2019 Long-Term Budget Outlook*, June 2019, 47. https://www.cbo.gov/system/files/2019-06/55331-LTBO-2.pdf.

12. CBO, "The Budget and Economic Outlook: 2019 to 2029," January 2019, Table 1, 2.

13. White House Office of Management and Budget, Historical Tables https://www.whitehouse.gov/omb/historical-tables/.

14. Provide bibliographic information.

15. Barack Obama, State of the Union Address, Jan. 25, 2011. https://obamawhitehouse.archives.gov/the-press-office/2011/01/25/remarks-president-state-union-address.

16. CBO, *Long-Term Budget Projections*, June 2019. https://www.cbo.gov/about/products/budget-economic-data.

17. CBO, "Answers to Questions for the Record Following a Hearing on the Budget and Economic Outlook for 2017 to 2027 Conducted by the Senate Committee on the Budget," April 6, 2017, 10. https://www.cbo.gov/system/files/115th-congress-2017-2018/reports/52523-qfrs.pdf.

18. Ibid.

19. Ibid., 11.

20. Quinn Brody and Torsten Slok, *A coming debt crisis in the US?* Deutsche Bank Markets Research, April 25, 2018.

21. Ibid.

CHAPTER 4

1. *Take the Three Week Challenge*, The Can Kicks Back, Dec. 4, 2012. https://www.youtube.com/watch?v=kjLujoEhsQg&feature=youtu.be

2. Kevin Cirilli, "Alan Simpson goes 'Gangnam Style,'" *Politico*, Dec. 12, 2012. https://www.politico.com/story/2012/12/alan-simpson-goes -gangnam-style-084627.

3. "'The Can Kicks Back' Launches Campaign to Mobilize Young Americans on National Debt," *PR Newswire*, Nov. 12, 2012. https://www.prnewswire.com/news-releases/the-can-kicks-back-launches -campaign-to-mobilize-young-americans-on-national-debt-1788629 81.html

4. Ibid.

5. Byron Tao, "Anti-debt group finds itself in red," *Politico*, Feb. 12, 2014. https://www.politico.com/story/2014/02/can-kicks-back-group -debt-bowles-simpson-103463.

6. https://socialsecurityworks.org/2019/02/13/social-security-expan sion-act/.

7. White House Office of Management and Budget, *A New Era of Responsibility: Renewing America's Promise*, Feb. 26, 2009. https://www.govinfo.gov/content/pkg/BUDGET-2010-BUD/pdf/BUDGET -2010-BUD.pdf.

8. Philip Klein, "Paul Ryan leaves Congress with his central goal unfulfilled," *Washington Examiner*, April 11, 2018. https://www.washing tonexaminer.com/opinion/columnists/paul-ryan-leaves-congress -with-his-central-goal-unfulfilled.

9. AARP, Audited Consolidated Financial Statements, Dec. 31, 2017 and 2016, 11. https://www.aarp.org/content/dam/aarp/about_aarp /about_us/2018/aarp-2017-audited-financial-statement.pdf.

10. Reps. Wally Herger and Dave Reichert, *Behind the Veil: The AARP America Doesn't Know*, March 2011, 29. https://web.archive.org

/web/20110406145610/http://waysandmeans.house.gov/Uploaded-Files/AARP_REPORT_FINAL_PDF_3_29_11.pdf.

11. Center for Responsive Politics, "Top Spenders" lobbying database, OpenSecrets.org https://www.opensecrets.org/lobby/top.php?show Year=a&indexType=s.

12. AARP Press Room, "Key Dates in AARP History," https://press.aarp.org/timeline.

13. See age data https://censusreporter.org/profiles/01000us-united-states/.

14. CNN Exit Polls, 2018. https://www.cnn.com/election/2018/exit-polls/.

15. Philip Klein, "AARP's Got Their Back," *The American Spectator*, July 22, 2009. https://spectator.org/41206_aarps-got-their-back/.

16. Washington Times, "AARP backs Medicare bill," Nov. 17, 2003. https://www.washingtontimes.com/news/2003/nov/17/2003 1117-115810-3771r/.

17. Jill Zuckman, "AARP: Don't mess with Social Security," *Chicago Tribune*, Jan. 30, 2005. https://www.chicagotribune.com/news/ct-xpm-2005-01-30-0501300337-story.html.

18. Patricia Barry, "Medicare in the Crosshairs," *AARP Bulletin*, May 5, 2011. https://www.aarp.org/health/medicare-insurance/info-05-2011/medicare-in-the-crosshairs.html.

19. David Certner, "Why the Chained CPI is Wrong for Social Security," *AARP: Where We Stand*, April 11, 2013. https://blog.aarp.org/2013/04/11/why-the-chained-cpi-is-wrong-for-social-security-presidents-budget/.

20. Mary Agnes Carey, "FAQ: Decoding The $716 Billion in Medicare Reductions," *Kaiser Health News*, Aug. 17, 2012. https://khn.org/news/faq-716-billion-medicare-reductions/.

21. "Seniors Lean Against New Healthcare Law." https://news.gallup.com/poll/123164/seniors-lean-against-new-healthcare-law.aspx.

22. Obama White House Archives, "Remarks by the President in AARP Tele-Town Hall on Health Care Reform," July 28, 2009. https://obamawhitehouse.archives.gov/the-press-office/remarks-president-aarp-tele-town-hall-health-care-reform.

23. Frank Newport and Jeffrey M. Jones, "Seniors Lean Against New Healthcare Law," Gallup, Sept. 24, 2009. https://web.archive.org/

web/20120925062254/http://www.demint.senate.gov/public/?a=Files.
Serve&File_id=d76988f8-332e-42f5-96b2-cf940c968688.

24. CBO, *Budget and Economic Outlook: 2019 to 2029*, January 2019,
Table 3-1, 62. https://www.cbo.gov/system/files?file=2019-01/54918-
Outlook-Chapter3.pdf.

25. Thomas R. Oliver, Philip R. Lee, and Helene L. Lipton, "A Political
History of Medicare and Prescription Drug Coverage," *The Milbank
Quarterly*, June 2004. https://www.ncbi.nlm.nih.gov/pmc/articles/
PMC2690175/.

26. Zack Cooper, Amanda E. Kowalski, Eleanor N. Powell, and Jennifer
Wu, "Politics and Health Care Spending in the United States," *NBER
Working Paper*, Issued in Aug. 2017, Revised Feb. 2019. https://www.
nber.org/papers/w23748.

27. Vanessa Rodriguez, "Among top lobbying spenders, AMA nearly doubles
outlays in second quarter," Center for Responsive Politics, July 21, 2015.
https://www.opensecrets.org/news/2015/07/among-top-lobbying-
spenders-ama-nearly-doubles-outlays-in-second-quarter/.

28. This was calculated using Office of Management and Budget historical
data from 1946 to 2018.

29. Philip Klein, "How George H.W. Bush's broken 'no new taxes' pledge
changed American politics and policy forever," *Washington Examiner*,
Dec. 1, 2018. https://www.washingtonexaminer.com/opinion/how
-george-h-w-bushs-broken-no-new-taxes-pledge-changed-american-
politics-and-policy-forever.

30. Philip Klein, "Why conservatives don't want to trade tax hikes for
promised spending cuts," *Washington Examiner*, July 8, 2011. https://
www.washingtonexaminer.com/why-conservatives-dont-want-to
-trade-tax-hikes-for-promised-spending-cuts.

31. Reagan-Carter Oct. 28, 1980 Debate - "There You Go Again." https://
www.youtube.com/watch?v=qN7gDRjTNf4.

32. Robert Pear, "GOP's Plan to Cut Medicare Faces a Veto, Clinton
Promises," *New York Times*, Sept. 16, 1995. https://www.nytimes.
com/1995/09/16/us/gop-s-plan-to-cut-medicare-faces-a-veto-clinton
-promises.html.

33. Sheryl Gay Stolberg, "For Democrats, Social Security Becomes a

Defining Test," *New York Times*, Jan. 30, 2005. https://www.nytimes.com/2005/01/30/politics/for-democrats-social-security-becomes-a-defining-test.html..

34. Mark McKinnon, "Harry Reid's Social Security Lie," *The Daily Beast*, March 28, 2011. https://www.thedailybeast.com/harry-reids-social-security-lie.

35. Michael O'Brien, "Reid: 'Leave Social Security alone,'" March 16, 2011. https://thehill.com/homenews/senate/150279-reid-leave-social-security-alone.

36. "Pelosi Floor Speech in Opposition to Republican Budget that Ends Medicare," April 15, 2011. https://pelosi.house.gov/news/press-releases/pelosi-floor-speech-in-opposition-to-republican-budget-that-ends-medicare.

37. "Granny Off the Cliff," TheAgendaProject, May 17, 2011. https://www.youtube.com/watch?v=OGnE83A1Z4U.

38. Sabrina Siddiqui, "Romney Attacks Obama Over Medicare, Obamacare In New Ad," *Huffington Post*, Aug. 22 2012. See also: https://www.youtube.com/watch?v=XbCsRsMUA5Y.

39. Philip Klein, "Hot new Republican attack on 'Medicare for all' will make socialism more likely," Sept. 13, 2018. https://www.washingtonexaminer.com/opinion/columnists/hot-new-republican-attack-on-medicare-for-all-will-make-socialism-more-likely.

40. Congressional Budget Office, *Estimated Impact of the American Recovery and Reinvestment Act on Employment and Economic Output from October 2011 Through December 2011*, Feb. 2012, 1. http://www.cbo.gov/sites/default/files/cbofiles/attachments/02-22-ARRA.pdf.

41. Barack Obama, "Remarks by the President and the Vice President at Opening of Fiscal Responsibility Summit," Feb. 23, 2009. https://obamawhitehouse.archives.gov/the-press-office/remarks-president-and-vice-president-opening-fiscal-responsibility-summit-2-23-09.

42. U.S. Department of Treasury, *The Daily History of the Debt Results*. https://treasurydirect.gov/NP/debt/search?startMonth=01&startDay=20&startYear=2009&endMonth=01&endDay=20&endYear=2017.

43. Naftali Bendavid and Carol E. Lee, "Leaders Agree on Debt Deal," *Wall Street Journal*, Aug. 1, 2011. https://www.wsj.com/articles/SB10001424053111903520204576480123949521268.

44. Bob Woodward and Robert Costa, "Transcript: Donald Trump interview with Bob Woodward and Robert Costa," *Washington Post*, April 2, 2016. https://www.washingtonpost.com/news/post-politics/wp/2016/04/02/transcript-donald-trump-interview-with-bob-woodward-and-robert-costa/?utm_term=.7dc074dd796a.

45. CNN Exit Polls, 2016, National. https://www.cnn.com/election/2016/results/exit-polls.

46. CNN Exit Polls, 2016, Michigan. https://www.cnn.com/election/2016/results/exit-polls/michigan/president.

47. CNN Exit Polls, 2016, Wisconsin. https://www.cnn.com/election/2016/results/exit-polls/wisconsin/president.

48. CNN Exit Polls, 2016, Ohio. https://www.cnn.com/election/2016/results/exit-polls/ohio/president.

49. CNN Exit Polls, 2016, Pennsylvania. https://www.cnn.com/election/2016/results/exit-polls/pennsylvania/president.

50. CNN Exit Polls, 2016, Florida. https://edition.cnn.com/election/2016/results/exit-polls/florida/president.

51. Shannon Pettypiece, "Trump Signs $1.5 Trillion Tax Cut in First Major Legislative Win," Dec. 22, 2017. https://www.bloomberg.com/news/articles/2017-12-22/trump-signs-1-5-trillion-tax-cut-in-first-major-legislative-win.

52. Philip Klein, "Republicans Repeal the Tea Party," *Washington Examiner*, Feb. 8, 2018. https://www.washingtonexaminer.com/republicans-repeal-the-tea-party.

53. Philip Klein, "Trump's phony budget relies on rosy economic assumptions and imaginary savings," *Washington Examiner*, March 11, 2019. https://www.washingtonexaminer.com/opinion/trumps-phony-budget-relies-on-rosy-economic-assumptions-and-imaginary-savings.

54. "Does the President's Budget Slash Medicare by $845 Billion?", Committee for a Responsible Federal Budget, March 12, 2019. https://www.crfb.org/blogs/does-presidents-budget-slash-medicare-845-billion.

CHAPTER 5

1. Quinnipiac University Poll, "Dean Leads Dems, But Bush Bounces Back," Dec. 10, 2003. https://poll.qu.edu/national/release-detail?Release ID=391.

2. Philip Klein, "Howard Dean Energized liberals in 2004, but he'd be on the right wing of the 2020 Democratic field," *Washington Examiner*, June 5, 2019. https://www.washingtonexaminer.com/opinion/howard-dean-energized-liberals-in-2004-but-hed-be-on-the-right-wing-of-the-2020-democratic-field.

3. Neil Versel, "Complete transcript of interview with Howard Dean, M.D.," *Modern Healthcare*, March 1, 2003. https://www.modernhealthcare.com/article/20030301/MODERNPHYSICIAN/303010725/complete-transcript-of-interview-with-howard-dean-m-d.

4. Transcript. National Public Radio's Democratic Presidential Debate; Des Moines, Iowa; Jan, 6, 2004.

5. Paul Krugman, "Running on MMT (Wonkish)," *The New York Times*, Feb. 25, 2019. https://www.nytimes.com/2019/02/25/opinion/running-on-mmt-wonkish.html.

6. Stephanie Kelton lecture, *But How Will We Pay for It? Making Public Money Work for Us*, Oct. 15, 2018. https://www.youtube.com/watch?v=WS9nP-BKa3M.

7. Eliza Relman, "Alexandria Ocasio-Cortez says the theory that deficit spending is good for the economy should 'absolutely' be part of the conversation," *Business Insider*, Jan. 7, 2019. https://www.businessinsider.com/alexandria-ocasio-cortez-ommt-modern-monetary-theory-how-pay-for-policies-2019-1.

8. Gregg Re, "Kamala Harris dismisses concerns about Green New Deal price tag: 'It's not about the cost," Fox News, Feb. 24, 2019. https://www.foxnews.com/politics/kamala-harris-dismisses-concerns-about-green-new-deal-price-tag-its-not-about-a-cost.

9. Philip Klein "Yes, Medicare for all is socialized medicine," *Washington Examiner* https://www.washingtonexaminer.com/opinion/columnists/yes-medicare-for-all-is-socialized-healthcare.

10. Philip Klein, "'Medicare for all' support is built on shaky foundation," *Washington Examiner* Jan. 23, 2019. https://www.washington

examiner.com/opinion/new-poll-exposes-how-weak-support-for-medicare-for-all-really-is.

11. Pew Research Center, "The Generation Gap in American Politics," March 1, 2018. http://www.people-press.org/2018/03/01/the-generation-gap-in-american-politics/.

12. Pew Research Center, "The Generation Gap in American Politics: Views of scope of government, trust in government, economic inequality," March 1, 2018. http://www.people-press.org/2018/03/01/2-views-of-scope-of-government-trust-in-government-economic-inequality/.

13. Steve Chapman, "Why millennials are drawn to socialism," *Chicago Tribune*, May 18, 2018. https://www.chicagotribune.com/news/opinion/chapman/ct-perspec-chapman-young-socialism-capitalism-20180520-story.html.

14. Marion Smith, "VOC Releases Third Annual Report on Generational Attitudes Toward Socialism in America," Oct. 30, 2018. https://www.victimsofcommunism.org/voc-news/third-annual-report-on-us-attitudes-toward-socialism.

15. John Holahan, Matthew Buettgens, Lisa Clemans-Cope, Melissa M. Favreault, Linda J. Blumberg, and Siyabonga Ndwandwe, "The Sanders Single-Payer Healthcare Plan: The Effect on National Health Expenditures and Federal and Private Spending," The Urban Institute, May 9, 2016. https://www.urban.org/research/publication/sanders-single-payer-health-care-plan-effect-national-health-expenditures-and-federal-and-private-spending.

16. Congressional Budget Office, *The Budget and Economic Outlook: 2019 to 2029*, January 2019, Table 3-1, 62. https://www.cbo.gov/system/files?file=2019-01/54918-Outlook-Chapter3.pdf.

17. Ryan Nunn, Jimmy O'Donnell, and Jay Shambaugh, *Labor Market Considerations for a National Job Guarantee,* Dec. 2018, 18. http://www.hamiltonproject.org/assets/files/JobGuarantee_FP_web_120318.pdf.

18. Elizabeth Warren, "I'm calling for something truly transformational: Universal free public college and cancellation of student loan debt," *Medium,* April 22, 2019.

19. Philip Klein, "Elizabeth Warren's childcare proposal relies on dishonest accounting," *Washington Examiner*, Feb. 19, 2019. https://

www.washingtonexaminer.com/opinion/elizabeth-warrens-child
care-proposal-relies-on-dishonest-accounting.

20. U.S. Energy Information Administration, Frequently Asked Questions: "What is U.S. electricity generation by energy source?" https://www .eia.gov/tools/faqs/faq.php?id=427&t=3

21. See "Green New Deal" resolution, Feb. 5, 2019. https://apps.npr.org/ documents/document.html?id=5729033-Green-New-Deal-FINAL.

22. Douglas Holtz-Eakin, Dan Bosch, Bem Gitis, Dan Goldbeck, and Philip Rosetti, "The Green New Deal: Scope, Scale, and Implications," *American Action Forum*, Feb. 25, 2019. https://www.americanaction forum.org/research/the-green-new-deal-scope-scale-and-implications/.

23. Elizabeth Warren, Ultra-Millionaire Tax. From campaign website: https://elizabethwarren.com/ultra-millionaire-tax/.

24. Letter to Sen. Elizabeth Warren from Emmanuel Saez and Gabriel Zuc-man of the University of California, Berkeley, Jan. 18, 2019. https:// www.warren.senate.gov/imo/media/doc/saez-zucman-wealthtax .pdf.

25. Lawrence H. Summers and Natasha Sarin, "A 'wealth tax' presents a revenue estimation puzzle," *Washington Post*, April 4, 2019.

26. Chris Edwards, "Why Europe Axed Its Wealth Taxes," *National Review*, March 27, 2019. https://www.nationalreview.com/2019/03/ elizabeth-warren-wealth-tax-european-nations/.

27. "Second citizenship & the migration of HNWIs 2000-2014," *New World Wealth*, July 2015. http://nebula.wsimg.com/33c082a103704a172b f3bd8d8288db65?AccessKeyId=70E2D0A589B97BD675FB&dispo sition=0&alloworigin=1.

28. Michael Rose, "Macron fights 'president of the rich' tag after ending wealth tax," *Reuters*, Oct. 3, 2017. https://www.reuters.com/article/ us-france-tax/macron-fights-president-of-the-rich-tag-after-ending -wealth-tax-idUSKCN1C82CZ?utm_source=npr_newsletter&utm _medium=email&utm_content=20190226&utm_campaign=money &utm_term=nprnews.

29. Josh Bivens, "Presenting EPI's 'Budget for Shared Prosperity," June 11, 2019. https://www.epi.org/blog/presenting-epis-budget-for-shared -prosperity/.

30. Kaiser Family Foundation, "Health Insurance Coverage of the Total Population." https://www.kff.org/other/state-indicator/total-populatio

n/?dataView=1&currentTimeframe=0&sortModel=%7B%22colId%22:%22Location%22,%22sort%22:%22asc%22%7D.

31. Philip Klein, "New Bernie Sanders healthcare plan is even more absurd than his old one," *Washington Examiner*, April 10, 2019. https://www.washingtonexaminer.com/opinion/columnists/new-bernie-sanders-healthcare-plan-is-even-more-absurd-than-his-old-one; For links to the actual bill itself as well as summary and supporting documents, see the bottom of the following press release from Sanders' Senate website: "Sanders, 14 Senators Introduce Medicare for All," April 10, 2019. https://www.sanders.senate.gov/newsroom/press-releases/sanders-14-senators-introduce-medicare-for-all.

32. Cory Booker, "Cory's Plan To Provide Affordable Housing for All Americans," June 5, 2019.

33. Elizebeth Warren, "I'm calling for something truly transformational: Universal free public college and cancellation of student loan debt," *Medium*, April 22, 2019. https://medium.com/@teamwarren/im-calling-for-something-truly-transformational-universal-free-public-college-and-cancellation-of-a246cd0f910f.

34. Press release: *Sanders, Jaypal and Omar Introduce Groundbreaking Bills to Ensure College for All and Eliminate All Student Debt,* June 24, 2019. https://www.sanders.senate.gov/newsroom/press-releases/sanders-jayapal-and-omar-introduce-groundbreaking-bills-to-ensure.-college-for-all-and-eliminate-all-student-debt.

35. Peter Suderman, "Elizabeth Warren's Plan To Cancel College Debt Is a Giveaway to the Well-Off and Well-Connected," *Reason*, April 23, 2019. https://reason.com/2019/04/23/elizabeth-warrens-plan-to-cancel-college-debt-is-a-giveaway-to-the-well-off-and-well-connected/.

36. Brian Riedl, "A Comprehensive Federal Budget Plan to Avert a Debt Crisis," Manhattan Institute, Oct. 10, 2018. https://www.manhattan-institute.org/html/report-comprehensive-federal-budget-plan-avert-debt-crisis-11497.html#notes.

37. Social Security Administration, "Contribution and Benefit Base," https://www.ssa.gov/OACT/COLA/cbb.html.

38. Richard Fry, "Millennials projected to overtake Baby Boomers as America's largest generation," Pew Research Center, March 1, 2018. http://www.pewresearch.org/fact-tank/2018/04/03/millennials-approach-baby-boomers-as-largest-generation-in-u-s-electorate/.

CHAPTER 6

1. Transamerica Center for Retirement Studies. *18th Annual Transamerica Retirement Survey: A Compendium of Findings About American Workers*, June 2018, https://www.transamericacenter.org/docs/default -source/retirement-survey-of-workers/tcrs2018_sr_18th_annual _worker_compendium.pdf.

2. *The 2017 Millennial Impact Report. Phase 2: The Power of Voice*, https://www.themillennialimpact.com/sites/default/files/reports /Phase2Report_MIR2017_091917_0.pdf.

3. "Millennials Less Likely to Be Married Than Previous Generations at Same Age," Pew Research Center, February 13, 2019, https://www .pewsocialtrends.org/essay/millennial-life-how-young-adulthood -today-compares-with-prior-generations/psdt_02-14-19_gener ations-00-06/.

4. American Cancer Society, "Cancer Death Rate Has Dropped 25 Percent Since 1991 Peak," *ScienceDaily*, January 5, 2017, https://www .sciencedaily.com/releases/2017/01/170105123106.htm.

5. Ana Sandoiu, "New HIV Vaccine Could Expose Latent Virus and Kill It," *Medical News Today*, April 9, 2019, https://www.medicalnewsto day.com/articles/324923.php.

6. Drin Duffin, "College Enrollment in the United States from 1965 to 2017 and Projections up to 2028 for Public and Private Colleges (in Millions)," Statista, last modified August 9, 2019, https://www.statista .com/statistics/183995/us-college-enrollment-and-projections -in-public-and-private-institutions/.

7. Evan Comen, "The Size of a Home the Year You Were Born," 24/7 Wall St., May 25, 2016, https://247wallst.com/special-report /2016/05/25/the-size-of-a-home-the-year-you-were-born/2/; "American Housing Survey (AHS)," United States Census Bureau, https:// www.census.gov/programs-surveys/ahs.html.

8. Josh Zumbrun, "Not Just the 1%: The Upper Middle Class is Larger and Richer Thank Ever," *The Wall Street Journal* (blog), June 21, 2106, https://blogs.wsj.com/economics/2016/06/21/not-just-the-1-the -upper-middle-class-is-larger-and-richer-than-ever/

9. "Iowa Household Income," Department of Numbers, https://www .deptofnumbers.com/income/iowa/.

10. "Fort Worth, TX," Data USA, https://datausa.io/profile/geo/fort
    -worth-tx/.
11. "Charlotte, NC," Data USA, https://datausa.io/profile/geo/char
    lotte-nc/.

CHAPTER 7

1. Author's calculation using data available at fred.stlouisfed.org, apply-
   ing the PCE Deflator instead of CPI-U-RS. For an explanation of the
   superiority of the former measure, see Scott Winship, "Debunk-
   ing Disagreement Over Cost-of-Living Adjustment," Forbes.com,
   June 15, 2015, available at https://www.forbes.com/sites/scottwin-
   ship/2015/06/15/debunking-disagreement-over-cost-of-living-adjust-
   ment (accessed August 21, 2019).
2. As he further notes, better government policies would probably have
   led to less compensation coming to employees in the form of benefits
   and more in the form of wages.
3. Lyman Stone, "Red, White, and Gray," American Enterprise Institute,
   June 2019, p. 25.
4. Bureau of Labor Statistics, "Quartiles and selected deciles of usual
   weekly earnings of full-time wage and salary workers by selected characteristics, second quarter 2019 averages, not seasonally adjusted,"
   available at https://www.bls.gov/news.release/wkyeng.to5.htm
   (accessed August 15, 2019).
5. "Retirement Throughout the Ages: Expectations and Preparations of
   American Workers," Transamerica Center for Retirement Studies, May
   2015. tcrs2015_sr_retirement_throughout_the_ages.pdf.

About the Contributors

———————— ⋛⋚ ————————

DAVID HARSANYI is a senior editor at the *Federalist*, a nationally syndicated columnist, a frequent contributor at the *New York Post* and *National Review*, and author of four books including his most recent book, *First Freedom: A Ride Through America's Enduring History with the Gun*.

PHILIP KLEIN is the executive editor of the *Washington Examiner*. He has written extensively on federal politics and policy from the nation's capital for well over a decade, and his analyses are widely referenced across the ideological spectrum. He started his journalism career in New York, where he was a financial reporter for Reuters. Over the years, he has written for or been cited by the *New York Times*, *Wall Street Journal*, *Washington Post*, *Los Angeles Times*, and *Bloomberg*, among many other publications. He has also appeared on television and radio, including on Fox, Fox Business, CNN, MSNBC, and NPR. He is a graduate of George Washington University with degrees in history and economics, and also holds a master's degree in journalism from Columbia University. He is the author of *Overcoming*

Obamacare: Three Approaches to Reversing the Government Takeover of Health Care.

RAMESH PONNURU is a senior editor at *National Review*, a columnist for *Bloomberg Opinion*, a visiting fellow at the American Enterprise Institute, and a senior fellow at the National Review Institute. He is a member of Generation X.